MW01232168

Wounds to Wisdom

Feel your pain, find your power, fuel your purpose

Lora Solomon MSN FNP

Contents

Introduction

Be advised, this book contains stories of violent events that may trigger painful memories or emotions.

This book is not intended to diagnose or treat illness. Please consult with your healthcare provider for medical advice.

"It is no measure of health to be well adjusted to a profoundly sick society." -Krishnamurti

We have largely become seduced by the false narrative of safety and security offered by today's healthcare system. Our allopathic approach assumes all symptoms are the enemy that can and must be managed and defeated. Armed with an ever-escalating battery of pharmaceuticals, "science," and medical procedures, the war against disease is waged. In this paradigm, there is little to no acknowledgement or respect for the innate intelligence of the body or awareness of the human spirit. Instead, there is an almost complete exclusion of our wholeness. I have been a nurse practitioner working in the United States for the past thirty years. My practice areas have included cardiac intensive care, emergency medicine, psychiatry, endocrinology, internal medicine, and functional medicine. I have experienced the increasingly devastating toll this materialistic approach has taken on myself, my family, my patients, and our species.

An All-Too-Familiar Story

During my younger sister Twyla's childhood, she struggled with fatigue and mild anemia. Although she had no specific medical diagnosis, she was chronically "low energy" and fragile. Twyla went to the doctor, as was required by the public school system, and got the regular checkups and mandated vaccinations. By allopathic standards, her medical history up to this point was "unremarkable." At fifteen, she went to the doctor complaining of heavy, painful monthly periods. They prescribed birth control pills, which did indeed seem to solve the problem—the heavy periods stopped. No consideration was given to the potential downside of manipulating a young woman's hormones, programmed by the body for precision release, or why her hormones were out of balance to begin with.

Twyla hated school but made it to graduation, and then to her first job as a bank teller. As a young adult, she gained twenty pounds and began suffering with symptoms of anxiety and depression, eventually making it to another doctor's office. They gave her a prescription for Prozac, a drug that impacts a neurotransmitter called serotonin, a nervous system messenger that affects nearly every organ in the body. Some years later, the mood symptoms worsened, and they gave her the diagnosis of bipolar disorder. The doctor prescribed another medication. Her weight continued to climb, while her brain function and energy plummeted and her relationships suffered.

In her thirties, as her emotional and physical health continued to diminish despite her prescribed medications, she began using "street drugs"—first marijuana, then opiates, then heroin. Her weight escalated, and she was diagnosed with type II diabetes. The doctor prescribed another medication. She then developed high blood pressure, which led to another prescription. Her ability to hold a job declined, and she qualified for a monthly disability check from the government.

Twyla became pregnant at thirty-nine, and during her pregnancy, she continued to use a combination of street drugs and prescribed drugs. In July 2005, she delivered a baby girl who tested positive for marijuana and opiates. Our sixty-six-year-old mother received a call from two states away. "Come to the hospital to take custody of your granddaughter or we will place her in the state's custody." Our mother sped to the hospital to take her drug-addicted newborn grandchild and daughter home.

Four years later, Twyla was told that she needed both a hysterectomy and a cholecystectomy. The heavy periods that had started twenty-five years earlier were still a problem, and they had newly diagnosed her with gallstones. They were both laparoscopic procedures, and she had them on the same day. She made it through the routine removal of her uterus and gallbladder, but died one hour later in the hospital. The cause of death on the autopsy report was exsanguination—she bled to death. When my mother considered suing for malpractice, she found that any monetary compensation would be based on the quality of Twyla's life. Given that Twyla was a known substance misuser on disability, she was considered of little monetary value to society. No lawyer would take the case, and it was dropped.

This story is not something that happened in a time and place far away from where we find ourselves now. This all occurred within the last few decades in the United States. The treatment that Twyla received was, and still is, "standard of care." It is an all-too-familiar story that I have witnessed time after time in the healthcare system. There was no part of her treatment, except for a possible surgical error, that the legal system would consider malpractice. She sought care from the healthcare system dozens of times, and she died in the hospital.

Systemic Issues

Early in my nursing career, I could see that the business of healthcare was not designed to restore health. People were not getting well—they were being managed. I observed that the system was primarily driven by fear and greed, not science. Frustrated by the "pill for the ill" routine, I decided I would get additional certification as a functional medicine specialist. This type of medicine, which touts itself as "root cause" medicine, trains providers to go deeper than symptom management. It requires advanced education in hormones, nutrition, detoxification, metabolic issues, and immune imbalances. It took seven years and 30K dollars to get the additional certification. I hoped I could finally experience the satisfaction of restoring health to my patients at a boutique practice where they were paying thousands of dollars for advanced testing and bagfuls of supplements.

Gradually, I realized the dynamics were identical. It was the same dance of perpetuating dependence on something or someone external. My patients saw their bodies as the enemy and their symptoms as something that needed to be eliminated. They were not being empowered or encouraged to tap into their innate wisdom or to trust their bodies. The ammunition was more holistic, but the battle against the body waged on.

This is the problem that we are facing individually and collectively. Nearly all healthcare providers study medicine because they genuinely care about the suffering of others, but I believe by the time they graduate, they are indoctrinated into ignoring the intelligence of the body and the actual science of how the natural world works. If they wake up to the dangers and inadequacies of the healthcare system, they are so in debt and dependent on the job that they feel trapped. Often only when their own health or the health of a family member cannot be helped by the system are some willing to venture out. Those who do step outside of the system are often ostracized as weirdos, wackos, or even criminals. Fortunately, there are more courageous souls than ever who are risking their livelihoods in order to speak the truth.

Human Biotechnology

The fundamental belief of the current conventional (and alternative) medical establishment is that symptoms are the enemy, and the body is the battleground for fighting the enemy. The economics of the system depend on you being sick, or thinking that your body is to be feared and disease must be defeated.

When I became ill and the system failed to help me, I began a decades-long exploration of how human biotechnology works. I am using the word biotechnology so that you may begin to consider the body as advanced intelligent technology. Twenty years ago, I began hearing the term psychoneuroimmunoendocrinology. Taking the specialties of psychology, neurology, immunology, and endocrinology and putting them back together. It was a new term that illuminated the truth of our wholeness. Although the healthcare system has taken the path of extreme specialization, compartmentalization, and materialism, this is not who we are. It is a misguided fantasy that only makes those invested in fighting with the body wealthier by the day. We have built a whole healthcare system on the myth of compartmentalization. There is not a single thing that happens to one of your cells that every other cell in your body doesn't know about. Compartmentalization does *not* exist anywhere inside or outside of you.

As a species, we most often live in the story that we are separate from each other and from life. Recently I began hearing a new term, bio-spiritual ecology, which is another way of trying to understand what saints and sages have been telling us for millennia. The ancient wisdom in the body knows that all life is connected.

When the blinders come off about the greed and empty promises of the healthcare system, it is natural to make the healthcare system the enemy and seek to fight it or change it. I will introduce you to an elegant solution that does not require any fighting with the system or creating of new legislation. If we see the healthcare system as a result of our consciousness, a different approach emerges. When we change our consciousness, the system will evolve. No longer will it be fueled by our fear of our own bodies. If we don't change our consciousness, we will simply create an updated version of the same old dynamic of fear and dependence. The solution requires that we understand who we are and how our biotechnology works from the inside out.

Does this sound too good to be true? Does it seem outlandish to think of your body as anything other than a stupid flesh suit prone to frequent mistakes in need of a healthcare system to defeat the enemy of disease?

You most likely have been conditioned to believe your body often makes errors and eventually falls apart completely. This has become the "accepted reality," but that does not mean it is the complete story.

There is tremendous wisdom and unlimited potential that you can access through your body. I want to introduce you to a different perspective, which encompasses both the ancient wisdom present in your cells and the modern science that recognizes we are part of something much greater. Often the words "ancient wisdom" can bring up visions of Egyptian tombs, Dead Sea Scrolls, or Sumerian clay tablets. The ancient wisdom that I am referring to is your actual body. There are four billion years of accumulated wisdom in the cells of your body right now. *You* are literally a book of knowledge. Your body holds the keys to this wisdom and is waiting for you to access what you know.

Symptoms are the body lovingly providing information that you are out of alignment or in the process of coming into alignment with life. They are messages from you, to you, about you, and for your benefit.

Your biotechnology makes no errors. Read that again . . . *It makes no errors . . . ever.*

It is precision technology that is constantly perceiving, processing, and providing feedback. I invite you to begin seeing your body as a constant love letter from the creative intelligence of the universe.

The problem is that most people do not know how to "read their own love letters." They walk around confused, frustrated, overwhelmed, and isolated while looking for some "expert" to tell them what test to do, what food to eat, what supplement to take, what mantra to chant, what yoga pose to sit in, what coffee to drink. People are looking anywhere except to themselves. It doesn't help that there are billions of businesses and many religions that promise us relief if we just buy their product or follow their ideology.

I want you to see your body as a technology designed perfectly to guide you into remembering who you are. You can go from confused, frustrated, and sick to clear, confident, and healthy without any type of "self-improvement" strategy. But how do we access this intelligence? How do we "read the book" that is our body?

After spending many years studying and learning about this ancient wisdom and correlating it with modern science, I am going to share my own stories with you and take you step by step on that journey with me. My sister Twyla did not have access to this type of approach. I would give anything to be able to share this knowledge with her, but perhaps it is because of her I am sharing this with you now.

As you read this book, I will invite you to go on your own journey of exploring the intelligence of your body and learning to translate your body's messages for yourself. I want to empower you with knowledge and confidence to claim your right to trust your body's intelligence. This is your birthright.

Don't miss out on the opportunity to align with the miraculous technology you possess while leaving your power and purpose unactivated. Don't spend another moment at war with your body, which is indeed a war with life itself and a war that you will *never* win.

Think of this book like the owner's manual you never received on the most advanced technology you can imagine.

This is my promise to you: In this book, I will crack open the doorway to a different perspective. It will empower you to see your body as the advanced technology that it is. You will be grateful for every cell and every symptom. You will never again discount your precious body as less than a vehicle for living your highest potential.

The purpose of this book is to introduce you to a different way of seeing yourself and relating to your body. Many topics and resources I cover may inspire a curiosity in you and a desire to go deeper. For this reason, I have created an online community, a course of self-study, group workshops, and the opportunity to work privately with me. For details on these offerings and access to many free resources, I invite you to visit my website, lorasolomon.com.

Chapter 1

"We shall not cease from exploration; And the end of all our exploring will be to arrive where we started, and know the place for the first time." -T. S. Eliot

Are we here by accident, whirling through space on a planet that circles one of a billion other stars? As sentient beings, existential thoughts such as these are ones with which we have all grappled. Unlike other animals, we seek meaning because we are conscious and, hence; we inhabit the world of our narratives. At one point in our history, we thought science would provide accurate knowledge that was undisputable, reliable, and could help us make sense of the world and ease our existential fears. We charged scientists with solving the mysteries of the universe. We believed that the scientific method could discover the genuine nature of our existence, and it did. But the scientists and we, as a species, were not ready for what we discovered. We are nothing less than the continuous offspring of love and life gradually becoming conscious of itself. To hold the paradox that we are both animal and divine was (and still can be) too much to understand with our ego based intellect. Yes, we are animals made of the dust of the earth, but we are born with the presence of the cosmic within us. Although we have continuously sought to separate science from spirituality, they are two sides of the same coin. *Spirituality is unseen science, and science is seen spirituality.* It is understandable that scientists have been unwilling to publicly admit this, but throughout time, many scientists have ended their careers as mystics. When they explored the science deeply enough, they ran straight into the mystery. We are being created out of the void by a benevolent intelligence that loves us fiercely.

Before we get too far into a conversation about the unknowable mystery, let's explore the mechanics of how the spiritual and the material perform the dance that we experience as a body. It is important to discuss what modern science tells us about our relationship with life if we are to understand our biotechnology.

Energy And Consciousness

First, we must acknowledge that *everything* is energy.

Whether it be a body, a plant, or a chair, everything in our physical existence is part of an interconnected web of electromagnetic vibrational frequencies that connects all atoms and particles in the universe. Vibration is the word we can use to describe the oscillating movement of atoms and particles caused by energy. As part of the web of life, the human body has its own vibrational frequency which is measured in hertz (Hz) units. This is the rate at which vibrations and oscillations occur. A cell in your body that is vibrating at a faster rate is measured at a higher frequency than one that is vibrating at a slower rate.

Your body came into being and like everything in the universe is continuously coming into being. Out of the void, there came a sound. When the sound began vibrating faster, there was light; faster yet, color appeared; and then finally the structures of the ova and the sperm that combined to create a form that developed into your body. The only quality that differentiates one physical thing from another is the rate at which it is vibrating. Your body is in a constant state of transformation. At the most fundamental level, and almost completely outside of your consciousness, you are experiencing death and birth in every moment. You are continuously being created out of the void. Since the time you started reading the beginning of this chapter, 300 million of your cells have died, and within the next twenty-four hours, 300 billion new cells will join your body. Tomorrow morning, you will not wake up with the same body that you went to bed with tonight.

Modern scientists have no difficulty with the assertion that all matter is energy. This is the accepted second law of thermodynamics. But what about the concept of pure consciousness and how this relates to energy and the material world? Source consciousness is a well-known concept to spiritual seekers, but most scientists have deemed this area of exploration "unscientific." It is the habit of science to discount something when it does not yet have the tools to measure it.

Source consciousness is known by many names, but the easiest way to understand it is to picture the cosmos as a light stream radiating out from a single point. The "big bang" that is still reverberating. It was pure consciousness that caused the big bang and set the cosmos in motion, and it is the full conscious contact with that source that is the birthright of every human.

This may sound like a grand impersonal idea, but in our journey through the body together, you will see that this is an intimate embodied present moment experience. It is the journey that is taking place right now in your very blood and bones.

We have been conditioned to believe that we are victims of illness—that our family history and events control the health of our bodies. With the modern science to understand that everything is energy and anything that can be perceived in physical form (like a rock, or a human body) follows frequency, it is clear that when we intervene at the level of energy, the form (including our bodies) will change as a result. When we become conscious of this, we become aware that we are not victims.

When we only intervene at the level of form, the best we can hope for is symptom management. Everything that we expose our bodies to will affect their frequency (e.g., air, water, food, sound, light, relationships, beliefs, etc.).

What does this have to do with your health? Your frequency determines the health of your body. Each cell has an optimal frequency for health, and when it cannot vibrate optimally, the cell's function becomes increasingly poor, eventually leading to dysfunction and disease.

It is important to realize that what we can observe in the body or the physical world is originating first in the world of pure consciousness and is gradually making its way through ever-increasing levels of density to become perceivable to our five senses. What we see in the way of symptoms is the end result of a long process. This is why treating effects (physical symptoms or the form) without exploring the cause (consciousness) doesn't bring full resolution. It is an endless game of "whack a mole" that leaves the pharmaceutical companies and hospitals richer, and you more dependent and sicker.

When we realize this, we know when something is out of alignment in the material world or the world of form, that the cause occurred in the realm of consciousness. In the current system, when there is a problem in the body, the furthest upstream that a scientist may look is somewhere in the physical form. So they blame a hormone imbalance on the endocrine glands or maybe a person's genetics. But what is affecting the endocrine glands or the genes?

When we *don't* look further upstream:

1. We do *not* find the cause and remain stuck in an endless and escalating cycle of symptom management.

2. There is a missed opportunity to expand our consciousness and take part in our evolution.

When we *do* look further upstream:

1. The cause is found at the level of consciousness, and the cycle of symptom management ends.

2. We are now in the realm of consciously taking part in our own evolution.

The Human Condition

We are born completely helpless and hardwired from day one for survival. Believing what our caregivers believed about themselves and told us about ourselves was essential for life. Survival is awesome. Without it, we wouldn't be here having this conversation. For most of what we learn in history class, this is where the story has ended, "Yay, we defeated the enemy and we survived,' but the goal of our species does not end at survival. The goal is a continuous expansion of conscious life, and our bodies are the vehicle by which this expansion occurs. All of life lives in the knowledge of cooperation and abundance, except for humans. Because we have an ego consciousness that tells us that we are separate, the future is bad, the boogeyman is out to get us, and we must constantly fight the enemy, we live in a story of fear. But the cells of the body are designed to thrive at a higher frequency than constant fear. The body knows that we are capable of more than simply surviving and is continuously inviting us to remember.

Biotechnology and Life Stories

Your five senses are collecting data every moment. Over time, this enormous volume of data creates unique patterns in your nervous system. These patterns become behavioral tendencies, then your identity or your personality. We have a perception of ourselves as "fixed," but as you now know, you are not the same person even from one day to the next.

When the body perceives data and presents it to the brain, the brain creates a story with the data. Your stories create a chemical reaction, which then causes an emotion. This emotion strengthens the story. Over time, you reinforce your chemistry through a series of unconscious stories and habits. This is your unique survival adaptation software, and it works as intended.

We all live in the world of stories. In a way, we are all living in our own conspiracy theories, although we each believe that our version of the story is the truth. Why is this important? Because we build each story on a belief or state of consciousness which has a frequency, and that frequency is the world our cells inhabit. Even in the same room or conversation, people are each inhabiting their own unique experiences (and frequency) based on their conditioning.

Bringing the stories to consciousness is a necessary ⊦ of using our biotechnology properly. The stories that we tell ourselves about our past and our future in the present determine our present-moment frequency and, therefore, our health.

There is an invitation from the body to honor our own history, our own survival conditioning, *and* create a story that allows us to go beyond what we were capable of even just one day ago.

Abundance and regeneration are our intended states of being. Because of life experiences, many of us exist in a survival state of lack and loss. This leads to constant fighting with our bodies, the planet, and each other. We can accept that in our personal childhoods and collective evolution, this must have been necessary. Yet when we cling to the narrative that survival is our life's purpose, we begin to self-destruct, and that self-destruction begins in our bodies.

There is a leap in consciousness that we are being invited to make, and our bodies are the vehicle for making the jump. The intelligence humming through your cells right now is the same intelligence that supports you in making the leap from surviving to thriving.

We have been conditioned to believe that the body is a stupid flesh suit that constantly makes errors. This could not be further from the truth. When you have symptoms in your body, you have unconsciously created them so that you may realize how loved you are. It makes sense that when you are sick or in pain, the last thing you feel is loved, but if you are willing to change your relationship with pain, you will be amazed at the power, healing, and potential to which you immediately gain access.

It is okay if you are skeptical right now. We are wired to avoid pain, and we create societal structures that offer the fantasy of a pain-free life. But changing your relationship with pain by changing your story about it opens a portal to power that you will understand and appreciate only after you have experienced it. In my work, I have walked with many people through this process, and the outcome is always far richer than they could have imagined.

When the body shows up with symptoms, we typically use the mind in an attempt to fight it or control it, thinking that we are separate from life, existing in scarcity, and afraid of the future. It makes sense with the unconscious survival conditioning that we would try to control the situation for safety and security, that we would grasp at anything to make the pain go away, not realizing that in the desire for escape, we trade our power and potential for momentary relief.

Given that I have already mentioned pain, you will not be surprised to know that the transformation journey of conscious evolution is not all sparkles, rainbows, and light. It can be compared to hospicing what needs to die while midwifing what is being born. If you have ever been present at a physical birth or a death, you know it's not pretty or predictable. Giving up survival programming requires that a part of you must give up its job of protecting you. Letting go of some of your stories can literally feel life-threatening, because your life did indeed at one point depend on you believing those things about yourself and life. But let's face it, being human is painful, messy, and unpredictable. We might as well claim the ecstasy of consciously taking part in our own evolution as our birthright and reward.

Becoming whole requires some unbecoming moments, and this is exactly why you need traveling companions. If we do this work in isolation (a mistake I have often made), the pain turns into unbearable suffering, and progress comes to a halt. We need each other to remind us to keep breathing when the pain is intense and celebrate when we step more fully into our power and purpose. Without support, the old stories will take over, and you can easily find yourself in a self-defeating cul-de-sac instead of on the open road of progress.

With the right support, you will tell yourself a story where your pain serves a purpose and expands your consciousness. Alternatively, you can continue telling yourself the story that your pain is unbearable, meaningless, overwhelming, and must be escaped. It is necessary to trust that you are strong enough to handle the discomfort. Surround yourself with people who have shown their own strength and can support you. I promise you—the pain is temporary, and you are so very worth it.

You were born with all the equipment you need to heal, transform, and evolve. As we travel through the body together, you are going to see how your body is elegant and precise. It is not your enemy; it is your vehicle and intelligent partner. You will understand why it is essential to cooperate with what life is showing you through your body if you want to find your power and fuel your purpose.

Although there are moments of pain, remember this journey is ultimately ecstatic. You are worth this labor of love, and all of life is conspiring for your good.

The Process

One method for understanding how consciousness and energy interacts with our physical body is through the seven energy centers. In this book, we will explore our biotechnology through the lens of these centers. With each one, there will be questions to help you investigate more deeply. Be sure to journal your answers to the questions related to each energy center before moving on to the next one. The energy centers build on each other, so you will have the most success if you don't skip any parts. Think of it as building a solid foundation before moving on. If you can visualize your energy as a pyramid, you want the base to be large. There will also be simple, yet powerful exercises that accompany each energy center. I encourage you to have fun with them and stay curious. You are the expert on you, so if anything I say or suggest doesn't resonate with you, trust yourself.

Going through the energy centers is not a "one and done" experience. What you can expect is a spiral process. You will go through the energy centers and do some excavating related to a particular topic, then need to go back again. You will always be expanding, so you will come back to the same conditioning again and again, but at a different level each time.

It is common for people to get frustrated with themselves when they see something come back, whether it be a physical symptom or a pattern in a relationship. Remember to move toward a place of trusting what is showing up in the present. Know that life itself is always supporting your expansion. Ask yourself a question: Do I want to use my energy to fight against myself, or do I want to use my energy to be curious about what life is showing me right now?

oint you feel stuck and confused, go back to energy center and see if there is a new layer of or a wound that you are ready to explore. Remember, you will revisit each of your energy centers many times as your consciousness expands and your resonance changes. This is not because of any fault on your part; this is simply the way humans evolve. Our "upgrades" happen incrementally.

One of the most effective tools you can start using right now is to begin bringing your stories into awareness. You will be amazed (and maybe amused) by the elaborate narratives playing in your mind. You can write these stories down in a journal or share them with a trusted friend or therapist. If you have never journaled before, know that there is no way to do it "wrong." Don't worry about grammar or spelling. Just get it out of your mind and onto the paper.

Let's do this together!

For a FREE downloadable journaling tool and a more extensive list of questions, visit my website: https://www.lorasolomon.com/freejournal.

Chapter 2

"This is the most important question a person can ask, 'is the universe a friendly place?'"
- Albert Einstein

Now that you understand how the current healthcare system cannot deliver on its promise of health, and are willing to consider the body as an intelligent biotechnology, we can explore a new way of seeing your symptoms.

In this chapter, we will begin the journey through the energy centers. Seeing the body through the lens of energy centers will help us explore and understand the language of our symptoms systematically. It will also help excavate and expose unconscious beliefs that we have inherited through our programming. Of course, we cannot divide you and your body into neat little boxes, so keep that in mind as we begin.

First, let me share the story of my mother and my birth as a means to explore energy at the very start of life.

Leona, my grandmother, lost her mother at age four and ran off with my grandfather Lawrence, at age fourteen, to escape her hateful stepmother and the beatings of her father. According to my mother, Lawrence was chronically drunk, jealous, and unemployed, but by the time Leona reached the age of twenty, she already had three children and felt trapped. As a woman in 1940 with no supportive family, education, job, indoor plumbing, or electricity, she had limited options.

My mother Nora was the second oldest daughter of Leona, who gave birth to thirteen children. The family lived in a three-room house perched on the side of a Morgantown, West Virginia mountain. There was a well for drawing water and an outhouse.They grew as much food as possible in their garden and had chickens and pigs.

There was a one-room schoolhouse that my mom attended through the fifth grade until they decided they needed her more at home than they needed her at school. When Nora met my father Joe at the local Pentecostal church, they both thought they were getting the better end of the deal. Nora was pretty, smart, and charming. She could whip up an impressive Sunday dinner and easily handled a room full of children. She was a church-going girl with a glorious singing voice. Joe had a job with his father in the West Virginia coal mines. He had grown up in town with indoor plumbing, was on his way to completing high school, and his brother had a car. They plotted an "accidental pregnancy" and were married at age 19.

Three weeks before I was born on a pleasant New Jersey April afternoon, my twenty-three-year-old mother walked to the Green Valley trailer park laundry room with Joey (my three-year-old brother) to wash clothes and hang them on the line. A short time later, it thundered, and the sky darkened. She was worried that it would rain on her clothes. Nora called my father, who was at his brother's house a short drive away, to come home and help her take the clothes down. He didn't come, so she walked over with Joey to take them down herself.

Later, when Joe came home, she asked him, "Why wouldn't you come home to help when I asked you?" First, he ignored her question, then when she asked him again, he became defensive. "I was visiting my family. You shouldn't have been bothering me." When Nora pouted, saying she was his wife and was his family now, he caught her by surprise when he leaped up from his kitchen chair and punched her in the face, knocking her down. "No woman is going to tell me what to do," he exclaimed. In his world, a man didn't hesitate to use physical force to get what he wanted, and he just wanted her to stop talking. My mother had learned from her mother that without social support or money, her safety in the world was limited, and three weeks before taking my first breath, I was being conditioned, too.

Like all human bodies, my body was perceiving information about the world even before I was born. I was being calibrated to match the energy frequency of those I would depend on for survival. Our unconscious beliefs about whether the world is a friendly place form in utero and before the age of one. This hardly seems fair. First, that such an important belief is unconscious, and second, that it happens at such a young age, but survival is paramount.

Before we are born, our life is supported through our mother in the uterus. When we take our first breath on our own, we experience separation for the first time and we become dependent on the external environment. Even in the best of circumstances, birth and separation are hard. We go from feeling completely nourished and held to being on our own. Survival adaptation is hard-wired at birth. Babies are born knowing how to get the attention and approval of their caregivers to ensure their survival. As helpless newborns, we have to hit the ground running.

The nervous system and unconscious mind of an infant will continuously condition itself to align with the frequency and the beliefs that are necessary to maintain attachment to its caregivers. This is the wisdom of survival already dialed in and ready to go.

The Energy Center Of Physical Support

The first energy center of the body is formed in the first twelve months of life and provides the will to live in the physical world. It also provides the platform for beliefs related to our physical security.

Our most basic chemicals, in response to the danger of being physically threatened, come from our adrenal glands. These walnut-sized glands sit on top of the kidneys and produce a variety of substances, including adrenaline and cortisol, which help to regulate blood pressure, electrolyte imbalance, metabolism, immune function, and sex hormones. In short, we can consider these our "stress response" hormones or our fight, flight, or freeze chemistry.

These glands constantly respond to the story of safety that the mind is communicating, either consciously or unconsciously. The body is continuously scanning the environment for information. Your brain brings in the data for review and asks, "Am I safe?" Given that we form these beliefs during the first year of life, it is the unconscious mind that is making the call. The adrenal glands respond to direction from the hypothalamus and the pituitary, which are found in the brain. These glands, based on all the information they are gathering from internal and external sources, will cause the release of the corresponding chemicals.

The brain is wired to read patterns in the environment and to repeat responses that maintain survival. So if a caregiver behaves dangerously just one time when they are angry, the brain will release danger response chemicals every time that parent figure is angry. Not only that, until we bring this to consciousness, every time another human who holds a position of power is angry, the body will release these same chemicals, and your body will respond in the same way that has allowed you to survive in the past. When a response to danger is successful (you survive), it becomes a "program."

Our programming also informs us that if our caregivers are not responding to our needs, that our physical lives are in danger. This is true for an infant. If your caregiver is unable or unwilling to provide shelter, food, and nurturing to you, you will not survive. Neglect is perceived as a threat and also creates a response pattern and a program.

In every moment, your cells are vibrating somewhere along the continuum of feeling completely supported by life or abandoned. It is the rare person who goes through every day from birth to death feeling totally supported. When the programming causes the energy frequency to consistently drop below what is necessary for the cells to be healthy, imbalance, symptoms, and eventually, disease will occur in the body. Remember, everything is energy, and the frequency of the energy creates the form.

We are born knowing we cannot survive alone. As you grow, you look down at your body and it looks separate from your family, your classmates, and the environment. You can see where your skin separates you from everything else. You have a gender, a name, and a personality.

Whatever beliefs are needed for physical survival, those are the beliefs that are wisely adopted by your unconscious mind. Once you understand this and look around the world at people's behaviors, you can see how these unconscious programs are playing out in their lives.

When there is a present-moment physical threat, the messages sent to the body help a person to fight or run away from the threat. If neither of these options is possible, your body will "freeze" or your mind will temporarily dissociate from the body to escape the overwhelming experience. This is essential because a real physical threat needs to be dealt with immediately. As adults, in our modern world, very few of us face present-moment physical threats, but our bodies are still producing the chemicals that are designed for that type of response.

According to the *Journal of the American Medical Association*, it is estimated that 80 percent of visits to the doctor are stress related, meaning 80 percent of our physical ailments result from our bodies producing chemicals to help us respond to a present-moment physical threat when there is no present-moment physical threat. This is how the survival adaptation morphs into self-destruction if we do not bring the beliefs into consciousness.

Most of our "threats' are ego threats or psychological threats, but our bodies don't know the difference between a poisonous snake or a nasty email. The chemicals are the same, and the body's response is the same.

There are many pharmaceuticals to treat the symptoms of living in a constant state of threat. For example, there are at least eleven different classes of antihypertensive or blood pressure medications, and in each class, there are over ten different drugs. High blood pressure directly results from constant threat signals being sent from the brain to the adrenal glands. There are no pharmaceuticals, nor ever will be one, that can permanently disconnect a person's consciousness from their own body without destroying the body. Pharmaceuticals can turn off the warning signal that the system is in self-destruction mode, but they cannot change the unconscious beliefs or stop the messages. If that were the case, you could take a blood pressure pill once instead of needing to take it every day. This is true for any pharmaceutical that needs to be taken every day. It is a clear sign you are not fixing the problem; you are turning off the fire alarm without putting out the fire, or managing the effect without addressing the cause.

One of the biggest mistakes we make is trying to use our minds to talk our bodies out of the stress response. This doesn't work because the older parts of the brain responsible for survival have a relationship with the body going back millions of years, while the frontal cortex that handles complex language is a relative newcomer to our physiology.

Because of my experiences while my mother was pregnant and into my first year of life, I became conditioned to a belief that I was not wanted—that my life was not supported. I am not saying that it was true, yet believing it was true provided me with a life-sustaining attachment to my caregivers. When my father came home from his factory work shift wearing his dirty blue uniform smelling of sweat and grease and collapsed into his recliner, I believed it was my fault he had to work at a job he hated to provide shelter and food for me. I thought that if I didn't exist, he would be happier. I believed what he believed, that the world was a mean place of scarce resources. Given my circumstances, it makes sense that I developed these beliefs.

How can a human go from the conditioning of "I am abandoned and in danger" to "I am supported"? How can the signal of safety begin broadcasting so the body can function appropriately?

The Mind-Body Connection

In healthcare, we have many labels for the chemicals our bodies produce. Hormones, neurotransmitters, antibodies, cytokines, the list goes on and on. Most of the focus in western medicine is to figure out where the body has gone "wrong" to the point of causing an unwanted symptom in the body and eliminating the symptom.

Looking through the lens of the body as intelligent and incapable of errors, when the body is producing chemicals that have become destructive, we turn our attention to the programming and conditioning for the error. Where are the errors in the programming? How can those errors be corrected?

When we recognize our conditioning and how, because of the conditioning, we have created a story about ourselves and life that has become self-destructive, it is understandable that we get frustrated with ourselves. Yet we need to honor our own ability, and that of our ancestors, to survive life's circumstances. This is not an excuse to stay in survival conditioning, but compassion is in order for our younger selves and our ancestors as we move through the process of deconditioning.

Most aspects of our modern society are built on the belief in physical insecurity and scarcity. Nearly every horrible thing that one human has done to another has been from this conditioning.

If we were truly abandoned by the source of life, this would be our only way to cope. We would indeed be in competition with all of life for our survival. Becoming conscious of how our physical insecurity is driving our behaviors is the first step in challenging this self-destructive belief. Evolving to a place of knowing that you are physically supported by life, that your very existence is proof that all of life is conspiring for you to be here, becomes the medicine that heals us at this energy center. When we bring this truth into consciousness, we give birth to a supported life, instead of a repetitive pattern of self-protection born out of the belief that we have been abandoned.

Allowing myself to be reconditioned from the belief of abandonment and danger is an ongoing process. Within the same hour, I may get a sense of being supported by an abundant life source and then worry about having enough money to pay the power bill. In my decision to give up a well-paying job that required me to prescribe drugs I didn't believe in, I experienced constant physical uncertainty. The most reliable tool that I have used to switch my body out of danger conditioning is breathwork. Changing the way I breathe allows my body to calm my brain and loosens the grip of the conditioning.

Becoming conscious of your connection to the web of life is the root of your power and purpose. Until the safety switch is *on*, your body will produce chemicals that are self-destructive. This is *not* an error in your body; it is old programming that can be corrected.

When you become willing to let go of the unconscious self-protection that has become self-destructive, you understand that although we are each having a separate experience, we are not, and have never been, abandoned by life. We are continuously being created anew out of the void, which is giving birth to all of life.

Time to Get Curious

Here are some questions to help you "read" your body and beliefs related to physical security:

- What do you know about your mother's pregnancy and your first year of life? Did your mother feel safe and supported? Did you?

- If I had an endless supply of_____ , I would feel supported in my body and life.

- How safe and secure do you feel in your body?

- How supported by life do you feel when you are trying new things?

- Do you have trouble managing money (hoarding or overspending)?

- Do you have trouble putting down roots, or staying in one place?

- Do you have frequent or chronic physical symptoms related to any of the following: adrenal glands, bladder, kidneys, perineum or base of spine, high blood pressure, anxiety, weight gain around the belly from excess "stress hormones"?

- What other aspects of your conditioning around physical security have occurred to you as you have been reading through this chapter?

What to do:

If you have identified that a sense of physical insecurity is having an impact on your life, the most powerful tool that you can begin using right now is breathwork. This will send an immediate message of safety to your body and is the foundation of many other effective tools. The simplest exercise I have used most often is the 4/7/8 breath. Inhale through your nose to the count of four seconds, hold the breath in the belly for a count of seven seconds, and exhale completely through the mouth for eight seconds. Try it for four breaths and see what happens. There are also several free resources available on my website.

Be sure to journal your answers to the questions related to this energy center before continuing. It is essential to gradually build a solid foundation as you journey through your body.

In the second energy center, you will discover how your conditioning may be impacting your ability to have healthy relationships.

Chapter 3

"Your biography becomes your biology." - Caroline Myss

Now that you have had time to explore the way your body communicates through your adrenal glands, we can continue the journey upward in the body to the organs of reproduction. After ensuring our basic physical security, we turn our energy toward our relationships.

A Story of Internalized Guilt

Now I'll tell you an even more personal story.

My father's brother founded a United Pentecostal church. This church was the center of our family life, with my grandparents, aunts, uncles, and cousins each playing their roles. We attended church every Thursday night, Sunday morning, and Sunday night. In addition, we often had social gatherings at the church. To give you some idea of how strict our church was, girls could *not* wear pants (pants were for boys), sleeveless tops, dresses above their knees, shorts, bathing suits, V-neck tops, open-toed shoes, nail polish, or jewelry. We were *not* allowed to go to the movies, sporting events, or dances. Alcohol and premarital sex were *not* allowed. Social contact with people outside of the family, church, and school was forbidden.

During the spring of my junior year in high school, right before my 17th birthday, I managed to get to a friend's house who was not part of the church. She had a brother two years older, and some of his friends came over to the house. I had my first sips of beer and kissed one of the boys. It was the most exciting thing that had ever happened to me. I was so thrilled with my adventure that I shared my activities with a trusted church member. She told my uncle, the minister. It was a late Saturday morning in April when my uncle called to tell my dad what I had been up to. We had one phone in the house on the kitchen wall. When my dad hung up the phone, he yelled, "Lora Dell." As he came down the hall, I was sitting in the small shared bedroom with my sister. She ran out of the room when it was clear that my dad only had questions for me.

I was wearing a green velour robe with a flowered collar that my aunt Donna had given to my mom for her birthday. We never went without the essentials, but it was rare to have anything luxurious. My mom wouldn't wear it because it was too fancy. I think she was insulted that my aunt thought she was the kind of woman who lounged around in a fancy bathrobe. It delighted me when she said I could have it. The robe was the nicest piece of clothing I had, and I wore it every chance I got. I was wearing the underwear that had the days of the week printed on them. I was very careful to wear the right underwear on the right day. I was not wearing a bra. My dad started by shouting questions. "Why did you lie about going to your friend's house? Did you drink alcohol? Did you have sex with any of those boys? You're probably already pregnant." I was trying to answer his questions calmly, but I was terrified and trying so hard to say something to make him less upset.

Within a few minutes, he took off his belt, grabbed my arm, and started hitting me. I was trying to hold the robe closed to cover myself, and the robe ripped. I tried to protect myself from the belt with the other hand while calling out, "Please stop." The belt flashed through the air, hitting my face, my back, my legs. It seemed to go on forever. When he left the room, I was lying on the floor, and I stayed there for about thirty minutes, afraid to move, not knowing what was coming next, not wanting to stand up and see myself in the mirror. Surprisingly, I didn't cry as I slowly climbed onto the bed to lie down. A few hours later, I went to the mirror to survey the damage. There were bruises and scrapes where the belt buckle had torn the skin on my legs, chest, back, and face. For the next twenty-four hours, I left my bedroom only to cross the hallway to the bathroom. I stayed home from school for a week so that I could hide the marks on my body. That type of violence was so commonplace in my house that it didn't occur to me to report it or get help.

Three weeks later, I took an overdose of aspirin in a suicide attempt. At the hospital, after the doctor removed the contents of my stomach and the danger was past, he told my parents, "A suicide attempt is a cry for help. I recommend you get some counseling for your daughter." My father replied, "I don't need a stranger telling me how to take care of my daughter." We went straight home, and my dad made everyone kneel in the living room and pray for God's help. I remember thinking God obviously didn't care about me, but I pretended to pray to keep my father from getting angry. It was after midnight and having just come from the emergency room, all I wanted to do was go to bed.

Ten years later, I began to experience chronic pelvic pain. I was in nursing school at the time and engaged to a physician, so I had access to the best doctors in Philadelphia. I had a few experimental surgical procedures, along with several "trials" of medications. One medication was an antibiotic that created an ulcer in my esophagus, and another was a medication that dropped my blood pressure so low that I fainted in the medical supply closet during my nursing school clinical. Neither the cause of the pain nor an effective treatment was ever found, but the pain gradually diminished on its own.

My father died a few years later, and just after his death, I began having ovarian pain. I had a pelvic ultrasound, and they discovered I had a cyst on my right ovary. The recommendation was that I take the birth control pill, but something inside of me pushed back against that suggestion. A few months later, while working my staff nursing shift in the cardiac intensive care unit, the pain came back with a vengeance. I told my manager that I needed to leave and headed home in my Volkswagen Jetta. It was a forty-minute drive down the interstate, and halfway home the pain was so bad that I had to pull over. I thought if I could lie in the grass at the rest stop for a few minutes, the pain would let up and I could make it home. I laid in the grass for about ten minutes, but every time I tried to get back in the car, the pain would bring me to my knees. Finally, I accepted that I would not make it home and went to the closest emergency room. Within an hour of my arrival, I was in the operating room having my right ovary removed. I had developed a "torsed ovary," which is when your body literally ties your own ovary in a knot.

Physical Impacts of Mental Programming

Now that you are beginning to understand how energy and frequency impact your physical health, you can see that my body could not function as intended because of my programming. The conditioning that occurred based on my experiences in my relationships was not allowing enough energy into my body to support healthy ovaries.

We are all relational. We know deep in our cells that our species will not continue without relationships. Because of what happened, I was programmed to carry the energy frequency of guilt so that I could maintain a life-sustaining connection with my family. I had developed a necessary but self-destructive error in my programming.

As we go deeper into understanding the intelligence of the body, you can see how the beliefs that I had about relationships created a frequency mismatch, leading to an imbalance in my hormones that eventually showed up as pain and dysfunction. Over time, it progressed to me tying my ovary in a knot. There is nothing that can grab your attention more than losing a body part. These beliefs were all occurring deep within my subconscious. It would be years before I became conscious of what was happening.

The body communicates with precision. When you view the body as a technology that does not make mistakes, then you can see that your symptoms are *always* messages from you, to you, about you, and for you.

The Energy Center of Connection

The energy center of connection affects the hormones of reproduction. We often refer to the hormones of this center as the sex hormones. A woman's ovaries produce estrogen, progesterone, and testosterone. A man's testicles produce testosterone. This energy center also affects the uterus, kidneys, and bladder. It is most deeply affected by events that occur between the ages of six months and two years. As children under the age of two, most of us were not exposed to things we would consider "sexual," but if you can see this as simply the center of relationships, you can have a better understanding of how the energy held in this center affects all of our relationships, not just our sexual ones.

Because of the unique wiring of humans and our need for relationships, regardless of what a parent or caregiver does to a child, a child will automatically perceive themselves as somehow lacking or wrong instead of their caregivers. If a parent does not respond to our needs or treat us well, we will automatically create a story that *we* are the problem, or *we* are bad in some way. This way of thinking allows life-sustaining connections to be maintained and lays the groundwork for a distorted sense of relationships. Children cannot understand or tolerate the reality that a parent may be sick, tired, distracted, inept, or overwhelmed. To accept a story of deficiency or lack in the caregiver would be too threatening to our need for care and connection.

Long before I developed sexually, I took on the energetic signature or frequency of guilt that the connection to my family required of me. This was well established and evidenced by the fact that I didn't ask for or expect any help from my family after the beating or the suicide attempt. I knew from many other experiences and observations any effort to get help would threaten my essential relationships.

In every moment, your cells are vibrating somewhere along the continuum of feeling completely connected or isolated. It is the rare person who goes through every day from birth to death feeling completely connected in all of their relationships. When the programming causes the energy frequency to consistently drop below what is necessary for the cells to be healthy, then imbalance, symptoms, and eventually, disease will occur in this part of the body.

During my teen years, I couldn't stop my body from changing, and I couldn't stay attached to my family as my sexuality blossomed. It was an impossible position. This type of double bind is common in families, knowing that relationships are necessary for survival and that being accepted is necessary to maintain the relationship. There is an unspoken energetic contract families agree to that, on one hand, provides the support of the individual, but also exacts a price for the support. Most people, at one point or another, have had to make a choice—become the full expression of who they are *or* maintain the acceptance (energetic contract) of life-sustaining relationships. This is the birthplace of unconscious self-betrayal in relationships.

All relationships have unspoken "energetic contracts." Some of these contracts are healthy and supportive, and some are not. If you experienced an energetic contract with your family that did not allow you to be your whole self, then your unconscious mind will be conditioned to a story that relationships are not safe to explore and enjoy in your life. So often I have worked with good-looking, successful people who find it impossible to establish healthy long-term relationships because of their programming—an unconscious belief based on experience that close intimate relationships are "energetically too expensive."

You may find yourself in relationships where you obviously don't hold yourself in high regard and then beat yourself up for being in a "bad relationship." Yet our survival conditioning will only allow us to have what is energetically familiar. No one gets to skip ahead of the "frequency line." Therefore, you can break up with the "awful" romantic partner or friend just to find yourself in another "awful" relationship a short time later.

The conditioning around our sexuality is often confusing, but we can't avoid coming to terms with it without experiencing consequences. This must be examined and integrated or it will pop up later in physical or relational dysfunction. Many cautionary tales exist of leaders in society who did not bring their relationship conditioning to consciousness and ended up in a sexual quagmire because they still carried and projected the frequency of guilt about their sexuality.

The wound of this energy center is created when we unconsciously lose connection to ourselves in order to maintain connection with others. In its most extreme form, this is identified in the world of trauma as "dissociation," while in less extreme forms, it is a self-betrayal of some sort. It is a wise and necessary coping skill when our survival requires attachment to people who abuse or neglect us. This al-based self-betrayal then becomes an unconscious pattern of attachment to others. If you have experienced a pattern of repeated betrayal in your relationships, some degree of unconscious self-betrayal is almost always at the root.

Fortunately, as with all of our wounds, there is an opening or a portal to reconnect with our whole selves when we are ready. This portal is where we have the opportunity to become conscious of the truth that we are in constant communion with all of life. It is not possible for us to be isolated. If you consider that thousands of species of bacteria live inside of you and over 300 trillion viruses are in your body right now, you are not isolated from life. Disconnection is not possible.

When we bring the unconscious conditioning about our relationship patterns into awareness and thank the programming for our survival, we begin accessing the power of this energy center and experiencing the higher purpose of our relationships.

Time to Get Curious

Here are some questions to "read" your body and beliefs related to relationships:

- What do you know about your life from the ages of six months to two years?

- I don't have enough_____ to satisfy my need for relationships.

- Do you struggle with maintaining healthy long-term relationships?

- Are you willing to partner in creative endeavors with others?

- Are you comfortable with your sexuality?

- Do you find yourself repeating patterns in relationships that are unhealthy?

- Have you been repeatedly betrayed or abandoned in relationships?

- Do you keep your word to others?

- Do you have frequent or chronic symptoms in the following organs: large intestine, lower spine, pelvis, vagina, penis, appendix, hips, low back, prostate, ovaries, or uterus? Do you have hip pain, sciatica, problems with sexual response, symptoms of impotence, or infertility?

What to do:

If you see evidence in your body or in your relationships that there is imbalance or dysfunction in this energy center, I recommend you begin using the tool of compassion—first with yourself, then with the other people alive in this very moment who are feeling alone. The paradox is that when we abide with the pain of our own lack of connection, and become aware that many others are feeling the very same pain, we are no longer alone in our pain. We have entered back into the realm of truth that we are all connected. It is essential to remember that the external world is the reflection of the internal. Our dysfunctional or absence of relationships with others is a mirror reflection of our relationship with ourselves that can only be changed from the inside out.

Now that you have explored the energy centers of physical security and relationships, we can take the next step together and explore our need for being wanted as unique individuals.

For a FREE downloadable journaling tool and a more extensive list of questions, visit my website: https://www.lorasolomon.com/freejournal.

Chapter 4

"To be yourself in a world that is constantly trying to make you something else is the greatest accomplishment." - Ralph Waldo Emerson

Having brought some of the conditioning around our need for support and relationships into awareness, we naturally arrive at our need for being fully ourselves so that we have something unique to offer.

The Power of Belief

I encountered several powerful experiences in my life that

changed me in ways I wasn't aware. One of those experiences happened when I was eleven.

My father was brilliant at building things. He could imagine something, draw it, and build it. I still have a beautiful wooden bowl with his signature on the bottom that he made in his high school wood shop in 1957. He constructed an elaborate pulpit from which my uncle delivered hundreds of sermons. One of my favorite things was to join him in the garage, where he would show me how to measure and cut things and give me minor jobs with which to help.

Every tool had a place, and he swept the floor of the garage each night. One evening, I was playing with his Stanley retractable tape measure in the house. I was curious to see how long it was and pulled it all the way out, but then there was a problem—it wouldn't retract anymore. All evening until bedtime, I tried to get the tape back into the chamber, but it refused to cooperate. I knew that there was no way of hiding it. My mom fretted about the broken tape measure. She didn't know how to drive, and there was no way we could get to the store to replace it.

My dad was working the 3:00 to11:00 p.m. shift, and he came home at 11:30 p.m. While he was eating his after-work snack, my mom told him I broke his tape measure. He asked her to get me out of bed, and she roused me out of a sound sleep and brought me into the kitchen where my father was sitting. "What were you doing playing with my tools?" he asked. "This is broken, and it can't be fixed." He stood up, took his belt out of his pants, and while my mom held me in place, gave me several stinging swipes across my legs. Then he told my mom, "Put her back in her room, and keep her away from my stuff." I laid awake in bed all that night, and I never hung out with my dad in the garage again.

When I was sixteen, I got a job at the local ice cream parlor located just a twenty-minute walk down a two-lane rural road from my home. I wanted a car, so I needed money. I showed up at the restaurant every day after my sixteenth birthday and asked for a job until they gave me one. My uniform was a white dress with a brown-and-white-checked ruffled apron. I loved everything about that job. Getting out of the house and having some freedom. Wearing a uniform meant I could fit in with the other girls. It thrilled me when my pockets were full of quarters and one-dollar bills at the end of a busy shift. About fifteen other teenagers worked there, too, and were always complaining about the rules, but this was the most liberating environment I had ever stepped foot in. I never felt so carefree as when I was at work. Plus, there was plenty of ice cream to eat!

After working there for about six months, I met Rick. He was gorgeous—tall, with jet black hair, huge biceps, and a sharp dresser. Rick was a mature five years older than me and a manager at one of the company's smaller restaurants. He covered for our typical manager every few months. Our usual manager had a caved-in chest, sloping shoulders, and bags under his eyes. Rick was hell-bent on whipping our flagship restaurant into shape and showing his boss what an excellent manager he was. Most of my coworkers made fun of him behind his back. He did things like make us clean out the ice cream freezer with bleach and a toothbrush. I thought he was awesome and put him on a pedestal.

During my performance review, he told me I was the best server in all the restaurants and that I was so much more mature than the other kids. He even told me I had leadership potential. I was so pleased with myself for gaining his approval.

One day, he told me I was pretty and asked me if I had a boyfriend. It was magical, and I spent countless hours listening to love songs and thinking about him. I would go for weeks without seeing him, but when he showed up again, my heart was all aflutter.

Right before my eighteenth birthday, he asked me if I wanted to spend some time with him on our day off. I had my '74 Camaro, and I was ready for an adventure, so I said, "Yes!" I snuck out of my father's house for our Thursday afternoon date. Rick told me it had to be a secret, so I couldn't tell anyone at work. I was used to keeping secrets, so it didn't strike me as odd. For our date, I wore a white dress and white sandals that laced up the leg gladiator style. I drove to his house, and we went to see the movie *ET*. It was the first time I had ever been to a movie theater. He put his arm around my shoulders, and it was two hours of pure magic. At the end of our date, we kissed, and I floated back home in my Camaro.

A few months later, I found out that he was out of work for two weeks for his honeymoon in the Poconos. He had been engaged to his highschool sweetheart the whole time. I felt ashamed. On top of the shame, I felt guilty about lying to my family and my employer. I thought I deserved to be treated this way because I was a bad person. Unfortunately, this was not the last dysfunctional relationship I had with a man but was just one in a decades-long pattern of tolerating shabby treatment because it felt familiar. On one hand, I was smart enough to know better, but with the layers of shame on top of guilt, I couldn't seem to do better.

Guilt and Shame

In order to feel safe, children must believe they live in a

fair world—a world where good things happen to good people and bad things happen to bad people. Living in the real world, where bad things frequently happen to good people, would be too threatening. So when something bad happens to a child, they automatically and unconsciously decide it is because *they* are bad. This gives them some sense of control, because then they can work on being better and have some confidence that the bad thing won't keep happening. It is excellent for short-term survival but terrible for long-term health. Thinking that we *are* bad is the birthplace of shame, and shame is a major contributor to emotional and physical suffering.

While the self-blaming lie of shame is not conscious, on some level, we know we are betraying ourselves, and we also know that betraying ourselves is wrong. This sets up a layer of appropriate guilt (for the self-betrayal of our child-self) on top of the (inappropriate) shame, which makes it confusing to work through later. It can be almost impossible to respond appropriately to healthy instructive guilt over bad behavior while at the same time feeling the shame of *being bad* that once was necessary but now is toxic.

My body was my only way out of this confusing quicksand. With your body as your guide, you can feel the energy of shame. It is the absolute lowest energy frequency that a person can feel. For me, it literally feels like the blood from my veins has been replaced with lead. It is dark, heavy, cloudy, constricted, cold, and immobilizing. It is the loudest "no" that my body can communicate, and I am well acquainted with it.

Guilt serves a purpose that we have done something wrong and need to correct it. Shame serves the purpose of keeping the life force out. It allows the necessary conditioning to enter and take up residence in your cells. In a dangerous situation, shame is essential. It can literally drain your vitality and make you appear less threatening to someone who has the power to destroy you. It is a wise, life-saving physiological response in the moment that turns self-destructive as part of unconscious programming.

The Energy Center of Individuality

The third energy center develops primarily between the ages of eighteen and forty-two months, around the time when children naturally begin saying, "no." It holds our perception of our identity. When a person has a healthy third energy center, they have no problem identifying who they are, what they stand for, and what they want in life.

It requires a foundation of feeling supported by and connected with life itself—worthy of existing as an individual.

The pancreas is the endocrine gland that is associated with this center. This organ has two primary functions; the first is to aid in digestion by producing enzymes to help break down your food. Second, it also has an important endocrine function that helps regulate blood sugars, primarily with the hormones of glucagon and insulin. Conditioning that affects this energy center most often shows up as symptoms in the organs of digestion.

This is the energy center that helps us to "digest" things that happen in our lives.

In every moment, your cells are vibrating somewhere along the continuum of feeling cherished by life as a unique being or feeling unwanted. It is the rare person who goes through every day from birth to death feeling completely wanted as an individual. When the programming causes the energy frequency to consistently drop below what is necessary for the cells to function, then imbalance, symptoms, and eventually disease will occur in this area.

Digesting our food and having a normal blood sugar level are essential to having a healthy body. When our conditioning is telling us we are bad and we are vibrating at the frequency of shame, we cannot accept life into our cells. We literally don't feel worthy of being alive. Not surprisingly, I have a personal history and long family history of diagnoses related to abnormal blood sugar. According to the Center for Disease Control and Prevention, at least 40 percent of those living in the United States have blood sugar imbalances.

The simple ability to say, "no," is necessary for you to express your individuality.

Another way to understand symptoms in the body is to view them as the way the body says, "no," when the conditioned mind insists on saying, "yes." Some people brag about how they successfully ignore their bodies, like this is a desirable skill. Certainly, in times of actual physical danger, prioritizing survival is necessary. In our current lives, this is rarely the situation, yet many people live in chronic survival mode, as evidenced by the amount of problems we have with our digestion and blood sugar.

We all need to be recognized as individuals with our own thoughts, emotions, and desires. To live from a place of authenticity with something of unique value to contribute is essential for physical health.

Conditioning around this center is related to being or wanting something that conflicts with what your family, culture, or society says is acceptable or possible. When one's individuality is ignored or ridiculed through subtle and not-so-subtle ways, this energy center is impacted. For example, the education system rewards only certain kinds of intelligence, and society values math skills over creativity.

When we are conditioned that our individuality is wrong or dangerous, that we have to repress ourselves to be safe and accepted, then this energy center cannot function properly.

When this energy center is functioning healthily, a person can collaborate and bring their individual gifts to relationships without aggressiveness. When it is imbalanced, one can become self-centered, competitive, and demanding. Desperate attempts at avoiding embarrassment can drive someone to be a perfectionist or workaholic, or become judgmental and controlling.

The fear of failure leads to the avoidance of trying new things or fear of leaving situations that you have clearly outgrown. Chronic indecision and being easily manipulated by others are also a possible result of imbalance here. The fear of not being accepted frequently leads to being codependent in relationships. These are all things that I have struggled with throughout my life. In my desire to avoid feeling shame, I have taken part in relationships that required me to suppress my wants, needs, and individuality. Nearly all the time, it was an automatic, unconscious survival pattern that I could not see while it was occurring.

When a person goes to the doctor, they are asked about their family history. Did your parents have heart disease, cancer, mental illness, and so on? We know we are a product of our parents physically, and now we are seeing more clearly that we are the products of their conditioning.

There were plenty of times I wished for different parents, grandparents, upbringing, or history. How do we transform the conditioning of our ancestors to where we no longer carry that frequency that creates illness in our bodies? There is no benefit in blaming our parents. Circumstances conditioned them for survival, and they conditioned us. It is our inheritance. Another way to say it is, "We are all victims of victims." The invitation here is to integrate our past into a more expansive now. Not by spiritual bypassing or pretending we are happy when we are not; but by recognizing that we have the power to be compassionate with ourselves. With compassion, we consciously change the narrative, and in doing so, the energy or frequency will change.

The very nature of evolution is exposing something of lower frequency, like shame, to something of higher frequency, like self-acceptance. So often we try to let go of emotions when the solution is allowing that energy or frequency to let go of us. When the energy of shame is exposed to the energy of acceptance, it vanishes like darkness exposed to light. It does not work the other way around. You cannot bring darkness into a room and extinguish a light. Remember, anytime we are fighting with our emotions, we are fighting with ourselves.

This is simple but often difficult. Let me give you an example. Recently, I made plans with my partner of fourteen years to have a Thursday morning date. He cleared his busy schedule and was looking forward to it. I forgot to put it on my calendar and scheduled a meeting with a client during that time. When I told him, he was visibly upset and became tearful. I felt an immense wave of fear and shame that was way out of proportion to what was happening in the present. I felt the impulse to get defensive or try to talk him out of being upset. Instead, I was able to sit with my shame while he felt his disappointment. In less than fifteen minutes, the emotions had passed, and we were able to continue with our day. This may not seem like a big deal, but if I had not developed the ability to tolerate feelings of shame, the interaction would have played out differently, and a lot of time and energy would have been consumed in the process.

Something miraculous happens when we will sit with our uncomfortable emotions and simply allow them to dissolve naturally. Within seconds, they lose their power over us.

Developing the discipline of cultivating curiosity and friendliness toward painful emotions is the key, even if it is just for a second before survival programming hijacks the nervous system. It makes sense that a three-year-old is powerless over their conditioning, but if you are reading this, I assume that you are well over the age of three. At some point (now is the best time), to be liberated from the programming, there needs to be a willingness to feel your way through the pain and allow for something new. The only way out is through. There is no bypass.

Over the past decade, there has been much more awareness of the impact of trauma. Yet, one of the disempowering messages of the "trauma informed" movement is one of protecting trauma survivors from things that may trigger painful emotions. This type of approach once again places a person's power outside of themselves and reinforces a sense of fragility and dependence. This creates a habit of using one's energy to manage the external world instead of discovering the internal power and healing that can only be found by facing the pain directly. If you have already lived through a traumatic event, you have the power to process the emotions associated with it. You don't have to live a diminished life trying to avoid "triggers."

About Addiction

When most people speak of addiction, they are referring

to an external substance or activity. Yet if you go enough into almost any addiction, you will find a per... .1 who believes they *are* bad, and they are feeling guilty for their own self-betrayal. When viewed this way, we find the roots of addiction in the mixture of guilt and shame. Sadly, the addictive behavior perpetuates the cycle. It is a hellish place to live, but there is a way out.

Accessing power and wisdom through the wound, not around the wound or in spite of the wound, is the way out. The wound of experiencing being unwanted becomes the portal to experiencing the truth that you are cherished. When you depend on confirmation from the external world, the confirmation that you are cherished can feel elusive, but when you consciously contact the truth held in your body that all of life has conspired to create you exactly as you are, then the cells in your body dance to a healthy resonance.

While it may sound enticing to experience full deconditioning or to be free of programming all at once, in actuality, it would be uncomfortable and confusing. Our biotechnology can handle and maintain only incremental upgrades. Doing this work with the support of a person or a group who understands and honors the process of transformation is essential.

It is important to be patient with yourself. If you have been living with limiting programming your whole life.

give yourself the time that you need to settle into a new way of being. Transforming from a person with a habit of self-betrayal to a person who practices self-trust will take some adjusting.

At the same time, be aware of resistance to the deconditioning. Letting go of survival beliefs *always* entails some discomfort, and it is human nature to want to avoid the discomfort. Some of these changes can literally feel like "life or death." Although you are reading this and processing it through your intellect, it becomes real only when it becomes your lived experience.

Don't take my word for it. Make a practice of checking in with your body as you are reading this book, answering the questions, and going through your day. You can practice feeling your own resonance. A relaxed body, clear mind, and soft heart is your body's "yes." A tense body, confused mind, and closed heart is your body's "no." The conditioned mind will often disagree with the body because it feels threatened. It takes practice to begin acknowledging and trusting your body's "no." The deeper your wounds, the more elusive it may seem at first, but I promise you that your body's internal guidance system is intact and waiting for you to access it. I have never met someone who has permanently lost access to the wisdom in their body.

When you trust your body and access the truth of who you are, the radiance of your real self begins to shine through.

Time to Get Curious

Here are some questions to "read" your body and beliefs related to your individuality:

- What do you know about your life between the ages of eighteen and forty-two months?

- Do you like the person you are?

- Are you dependent on approval from others to feel secure?

- When did you stop believing you could be who you wanted to be?

- What story about yourself would you need to release to let life give you another chance?

- Do you feel justified imposing your opinion on others "for their own good"?

- Do you feel confident making choices that are in alignment with your values?

- Do you have difficulty standing up for yourself?

- Do you find it easier to compete than to collaborate?

- How often do you numb emotions with food, drugs, distractions, and busyness?

- Do you find yourself codependent in relationships, having trouble saying "no"?

- Do you stay in bad situations (jobs or relationships) out of fear of the unknown?

- Do you have any of the following physical symptoms: insulin resistance, diabetes, chronic bloating, food intolerances, gallstones, indigestion, pancreatitis, liver dysfunction, eating disorders?

What to do:

If you have identified that this is an area of potential healing, try the "should" exercise. Make a list at the end of the day of things that you did because they were what you "should" do. You can also have some fun with noticing when other people tell you what you "should" do. The frequent "shoulding" that we do to ourselves and others begins to bring the conditioning of self-betrayal to consciousness. Replace "should" with, "I could if I really wanted to." It is not realistic to go from living a life of "shoulds" to stepping fully into the power of your individuality, so this is a good place to start the exploration.

We will continue to build on the solid foundation of knowing that life supports you, you are in a relationship with all of life, and the universe cherishes your individuality. I trust you are excited to continue this journey and step into the power of your heart.

Chapter 5

"Someday, after mastering the winds, the waves, the tides and gravity, we shall harness the energies of the heart, and then, for a second time in the history of the world, we will have discovered fire." - Pierre Teilhard De Chardin

Now that you are seeing the relationship of the unconscious mind and the body, let's move a little higher to a fourth region of the body. This next energy center is an important bridge to the higher centers.

It is essential to be aware of the conditioning in the first three before moving on. For example, if you have a lot of conditioning about physical insecurity in the first energy center, it will be difficult for you to explore the unconditional self-love into which this energy center will invite you. If you have fully explored the questions leading up to this part and have experimented with some of the tools, then you can ask your body if you are ready to move on to this energy center. Although I am sharing the details of my own journey and a roadmap that has worked for many others, remember that *you* are the expert on *you*.

In my experience, this is where your relationships will change, and some loss may occur. I am not telling you this to scare you, but to help you understand and avoid the trap of staying in relationships that are no longer healthy.

One way to think about relationships is like seedlings that are planted in a pot. With the right conditions, the plants grow and thrive, eventually outgrowing the pot. Some relationships tolerate being repotted in a new container, and they continue to thrive and grow. Sometimes people are not ready to let go of their old containers, or maybe they grow in a different direction and are no longer compatible. This is completely natural, and there is nothing to be gained from judging yourself or others when relationships end.

Honor the relationships that make the transition along with those that do not. All relationships are precious.

You Can't Escape Pain Indefinitely

Now let me tell you a little about how I came to my darkest point.

Growing up, my parents did not allow animals in the house. We had hunting dogs that stayed outside, and for a brief time we had chickens, but it was clear that animals belonged outside.

My sister Twyla and I wanted to bring an animal inside in the worst way. Sometimes, when my dad was at work, we would sneak one of the beagles in the house for a few minutes, but never for very long. We knew there would be big trouble if Dad ever found out.

One day when I was about thirteen, a small gray-and-white-striped kitten started coming around the house. Twyla and I were so excited and snuck food to it every day. We wrapped it in blankets, carried it like a baby, and played house with it. After about a week, I noticed something odd in its fur. I looked closer—there were worms coming through the kitten's skin.

Shocked and horrified, I went to work trying to figure out what was going on with the kitten. Thinking that if I could pull the worms out the kitten would be okay, I took the kitten to my bedroom, armed with the only medical supplies I could find in the house: hydrogen peroxide, rubbing alcohol, and tweezers. I tried over and over to grasp the tiny illusive white worms and pull them out, but they would quickly slip out of reach. The kitten didn't seem to mind, so I kept at it.

I was so focused on the task at hand that I lost track of time. The kitten was still in the house when my dad came home from work. My brother told him I had the kitten inside, and I heard him yell at my brother, "Go get it and bring it here." My heart sank as I looked down at the kitten. I knew this would not end well. When my brother came into the room, I handed it over without resistance. I knew better than to argue with my dad . . . about anything . . . . ever. My dad took one look at the worms and told my brother, "Shoot it and put it in the ground." My brother was sixteen and loved nothing more than having something to shoot. There was no way I could avoid hearing the gunshot ringing loudly outside my bedroom window.

Fifteen minutes later, it was dinnertime, and I had to put a smile on my face. Seeing me sad would be another trigger for my father's rage.

I felt responsible for the kitten's death. If I hadn't brought it in the house, it would still be alive. I loved the kitten, and because of me, it was dead. This is how conditioning happens, but this is not the end of how my survival adaptation continued to impact my life.

When I was twenty-six, I fell in love with a handsome, Jewish scientist who was also an atheist (in some sects of Judaism, atheism is accepted). It was perfect. Finally, I was experiencing some real distance from my frightening, fundamental Christian nightmare of a childhood. I felt like the luckiest woman alive, like the princess who had been saved by her prince. After a lifetime of feeling trapped in a backward small town, I was going to Paris, France, for my honeymoon!

We married, moved to another state, and started a brand-new life. An antidepressant managed my occasional episodes of deep sadness and rage, and I was good to go. Until I wasn't.

When the chronic pain came back again in my late thirties and all the doctors and prescriptions in the world couldn't fix me, I started to explore spirituality. First, I started with a meditation class, then I began learning about the energy centers in the body, then I explored Reiki, Jewish mysticism, healing touch, yoga and shamanic practices, and more. I tried sharing these things with my husband, inviting him to classes and events, but he was annoyed and suggested that I was getting a little too woo-woo for him. This version of me was not what he signed up for and not something in which he was interested. When he saw I purchased a Buddha statue, placed it in the foyer, and set up a small altar in my closet, he was not happy. He tried to get me more interested in tennis at the country club or golf, but my heart just wasn't in it, and my explorations became a wedge between us.

I could either continue into the deep woods of the unknown and all the messy emotions in search of my wholeness, or I could escape to the known landscape of the perfect life I had created: the big house and the country club, the A-list group of friends, the good job, the family, my two daughters, the nanny, the international vacations.

For a few years, I tried desperately to keep a foot in both worlds—and became more exhausted by the day. It was getting nearly impossible to keep up the facade. I loved my husband and the security of my life, but I knew I needed to face the darkness inside and that I couldn't keep living a double life. I knew I could not keep up the "act" and do the work I needed to do. I needed to unpack the pain I thought I had escaped.

It actually took a brief and bewildering period of questioning my sexual orientation to blow the whole thing up. I mistakenly interpreted powerful feelings toward another woman as romantic and sexual when, in fact, it was me awakening to a more complete version of myself. When the marriage ended, I was back in a familiar place—believing in my conditioning that love is dangerous, and just like the kitten, I was to blame for the death of something that I loved. The guilt and shame were constant and suffocating.

During one tearful conversation, my husband said, "What we had was perfect, and you have ruined it."

But it wasn't perfect. Not for me. It was the perfect escape from my past and from myself, but it was costing me. To have that escape, I had to run from myself, and the pain in my body was letting me know I couldn't do that anymore.

People who thought they knew me were confused about the changes happening in my life. I had been so convincing in my "act" that my life looked perfect from the outside. I didn't want to know the real me, and I didn't want anyone else to know me, either. When it all came crashing down, I was completely alone. I could escape from my family, I could escape from the past, I could escape from religion, but I couldn't escape from myself.

The Power of Love

Love might be the most misunderstood aspect of the human experience. We are taught from an early age that love is something that we get or give based on conditions. If we are a certain way, then people love us, and if they are a certain way, we love them. This understanding of love could not be more self-destructive or further from the truth.

Our conditioning about love is understandable. Our parents told us they loved us (maybe) but then withheld their affection or punished us if our behavior did not meet their expectations. By the time we are five years old, we are conditioned to a version of love that we carry into our teen and adult years. We are unconsciously caught in the trap of trying to get love from outside ourselves.

The survival programming I unconsciously adopted was that love is dangerous. Love itself would put me and the object of my love in danger, and it is safer not to love. In fact, the opposite is true. Love is our path to wholeness, not something that seeks to destroy us.

I was also conditioned to the fantasy that I could and should manage the emotions of those for whom I cared. I needed to be in control in order to be safe. Naturally I became an expert chameleon and people pleaser, constantly scanning the environment, seeing who was in charge and what that person wanted of me. This conditioning served me well. In my home life, I believe it may have saved my life, or at least it saved me from a few beatings. It was much more important to be aware of and responsive to the moods of my father than it was to be aware of myself. Indeed, to be aware of myself was dangerous.

When we can transform our relationship with love from something that we need to control or something that we need to "get" or "give," we open the door to finding that love is who we are. The love we feel for others is ours, and there is nothing they can do to take that away from us. We can begin to function at the frequency of love for which our bodies are designed.

There have been many moments in my life that I have been hard-hearted out of habit and fear, afraid that the rejection or loss I would experience would be too much to bear. Unconsciously, I was guarding my heart from the frequency that it needed to function well.

Carrying armor around my heart and hiding my emotions was a survival adaptation. I was conditioned to suppress the anger and the sadness and put on a cheerful or calm face no matter what I was really feeling. As an adult seeking to have authentic relationships, this survival programming has created all manner of trouble. I know my unconscious behaviors have confused and wounded people who have tried to have relationships with me over the years.

Energy Center Of Love

The energy center of love is located in the heart region, and it develops between four and seven years of age. This center innervates the thymus gland, which is vital for your immune system function. The thymus gland handles the production of T-cells, which regulate the immune system by attacking invading organisms and providing immunity. T-cells also have innate intelligence; they "eavesdrop" on the internal language and let the subconscious know how to support the physical body. During our adolescence, as less energy comes into the thymus gland, this energy center begins closing down. As the frequency drops, your thymus gland doesn't secrete as much of the immune system hormones which are in peak production in your childhood and teenage years.

Even conventional scientists recognize that autoimmune diseases—where the immune system attacks its own proteins, mistaking them for a foreign substance—have an emotional link and are not simply because of physical or environmental causes.

In current western medicine, the thymus gets very little attention because it shrivels during your teen years and is essentially nonfunctional in most people by the age of twenty-five. In ancient cultures and spiritual traditions, they consider the thymus gland to be the residence of unconditional love.

At every moment, your cells are vibrating somewhere along the continuum of knowing you are fiercely loved or believing that you are unlovable. I have never met a person who has lived every day from birth feeling continuously loved. When the programming causes the energy frequency to consistently drop below what is necessary for the cells to function optimally, imbalance, symptoms, and eventually disease will occur in this center. If you are programmed to believe that you are unlovable, it is only a matter of time before this will affect your physical health.

Our breath and heartbeat are the very flow of life. When there is a lack of energy or low frequency in this part of the body, it will show up in a variety of ways—for example, symptoms such as shortness of breath, chest pains, coughing, asthma, or shoulder pain. Circulation problems, heart disease, frequent colds, bronchitis, breast cancer, pneumonia, or immune system imbalances can also occur. With heart disease being the number one cause of death in the United States, it is no secret where the biggest energy blocks live in our bodies.

In my work, I have used a biofeedback technology called heart math for over twenty years. This simple tool can now be used with a smartphone and an inexpensive ear sensor that gives you feedback on your heart rate variability and your state of coherence. This technology has shown me repeatedly how much control we have over the energy flow in our hearts. Simply cultivating a feeling of gratitude allows the energy to move and expand within seconds of focused attention. You can do this right now. Stop reading and bring to mind something that you are grateful for. It can be as simple as the fact that your heart is beating in your chest. Visualize the power of gratitude raising your frequency and feel gratitude for your ability to engage this power whenever you choose.

The heart is the most powerful oscillating frequency of our biotechnology. The magnetic resonance of the heart is 5,000 times more powerful than the brain, and the electrical output of the heart reads 100 times higher than the brain. It is the metronome to which the rest of the body marches. If you constrict your heart, the entire system enters discordance. If the heart is open, the entire system enters coherence. Discordance creates disease, and coherence creates health.

Most of us were conditioned to avoid feeling sad and angry. Not allowing sadness and anger to flow freely creates the experience of being stuck in emotional states that we label anxiety and depression. An emotion that meets no resistance has about a ninety-second lifespan. So, if a person is stuck in a feeling state for days, weeks, and months, it results from resistance created by unconscious conditioning.

With the invention of antidepressants, many believed a lack of certain neurotransmitters causes depression, but although a change in body chemistry may occur, the cause of any physical imbalance is found in your frequency. One of the biggest disservices that we do to ourselves and others is to encourage them to fight their emotions. Emotions are literally energy in motion, and energy is meant to be in motion.

Were you ever told by your parents, "Stop crying, or I'll give you something to cry about." If you have raised children, you can understand this. It is hard to see your child sad or angry—hard because most of us haven't been able to adequately tolerate our own feelings. So what do we do? We punish children for having emotions. We essentially punish them for having bodies, then wonder why they abuse their bodies. What we *can* do for our children is show them how we nurture ourselves when we are feeling emotional pain. They do not need to be our emotional support system, but they can handle seeing us upset and taking responsibility for ourselves. Where else are they going to learn how to do this in a self-nurturing manner?

One of the biggest lies that I have told myself in my life is, "I can't handle loss." I know this came from having losses early in life that I couldn't handle. They were too big, and I had no one to help me, so I had to tuck them away to "handle" later. There is a saying, "If you're hysterical, it's historical." I have often experienced emotions that are completely out of proportion to what is happening in the present moment. A minor disagreement with a close friend can feel life-threatening. I used to have many self-destructive ways to manage this, from just avoiding close

friendships altogether, being a people-pleaser, or b
off friendships when even the slightest conflict was on
the horizon. Now I have tools that allow me to use these
painful moments to do some reprogramming. Some of the
tools I have already shared with you. Breathwork, journaling, heart math, self-compassion. These are all resources
that create the space for me to "hold" these emotions for
myself with curiosity while the program is being updated.

This is the power of this energy center. It is the ability to
expand infinitely around emotions. We are programmed
that we must destroy "the enemy," but violence never
fixes, heals, or mends anything. It only destroys. This is
the mistake we have made so often in healthcare. Nearly
every treatment is "anti" something: antihypertensive, antidepressant, antianxiety, anti-inflammatory, antibacterial,
"fighting cancer." Our habit of being "against" anything
we don't like is baked into the system. Our very breath,
heartbeat, and immunity rely on our ability to allow emotions to flow freely through the body.

This energy center invites us to open wide and say yes
to everything that is—to stop the habit of self-betrayal
and self-destruction. Recognizing the futility in fighting
with something that has already happened takes courage.
We idolize fighting and war as courageous, but the most
courageous action is to sit next to your "emotions dis-
guised as the enemy" and accept that they are worth-

life. Life has created them special for you, so you can heal and expand.

The first and most difficult person for us to love open heartedly is ourselves. This means opening our hearts to actually feeling our own pain, expanding our hearts when the pain comes instead of closing them down. This requires a *lot* of courage and at least a little faith in your equipment, but your technology is build for change and with the proper care and assistance, it won't break.

The body is where this truce starts. We cannot skip making peace with our bodies and think we can have peace with our friends, family, neighbors, or other countries. The body is ground zero.

If you find yourself wanting to "destroy your enemy," it is because you are in conflict with some part of yourself. Every relationship is a mirror of how well you are loving yourself.

Loving another unconditionally does not mean agreeing with them. It simply means knowing that they are as worthy of life and of love as you are. It is noticing all of the ways you justify, argue, defend, and explain yourself so you can prove that you are worthy of love. You can stop. The truth has always been that you are worthy of love.

Our conditioning is part of what connects us with many of the most important people in our lives. When we no longer behave according to unspoken contracts, relationships will change, and some may end. Grief is an unavoidable part of the deconditioning process. Resistance to the fear, sadness, and anger that grief requires can be the biggest barrier to your transformation. It can feel like attending a thousand funerals of who you used to be and allowing others to do the same. I want to encourage you that you are worth whatever grief or loss happens as you become whole.

This is another place on the journey where you will benefit greatly from having guides, mentors, or those who understand the terrain. When you look back, you will see that any loss pales in comparison to what you have gained, and every relationship serves a purpose.

I have often been guilty of wanting a "spiritual bypass," wanting to skip the sad or frightening parts of my transformation through intellectualizing, blaming others, or wanting to have my programming whisked away by a knight in shining armor or a shaman instead of taking responsibility for myself. When I look back at my marriage, I can see I believed that the right husband, house, friends, and job would keep me from having to accept the parts of myself that I had unconsciously abandoned long ago. I was wrong, and as challenging as it has been (and still is at times), I am so grateful for the ongoing opportunity to become who I was always meant to be and walk with others while they are doing the same.

operates with cooperation, and as humans, we
through accepting our role. We are uniquely
designed to function best at the frequency of love. All of
life sees potential in us and is supporting us in claiming
our birthright as the continuous offspring of love and life
gradually becoming conscious of itself.

We recognize it in our bodies because our bodies are
built for this resonance. It feels like a blissful homecoming.

Time to Get Curious

Here are some questions to "read" your body and beliefs
related to love:

- What do you know about your life from the ages of
four to seven?

- Do you struggle with emotional neediness, believing that love is outside of you?

- Do you feel unlovable?

- Do you find yourself in power struggles, keeping
score with those close to you?

- Do you frequently feel lonely or cut off from love?

- Do you find it easier to please others than to please yourself?

- Do you struggle with jealousy?

- Do you have a list of resentments toward yourself or others?

- Do you use emotional wounds to control people or situations?

- Who would you be without the need to protect yourself from loss?

Do you have physical symptoms in any of these parts of your body: heart, lungs, circulatory system, arms, hands, breasts, shoulders and upper back, blood, immune system, or thymus gland?

What to do:

If you notice that this energy center is problematic for you. I invite you to try a simple exercise. For a few days, list all the emotions that you have without censoring them. You don't need to write the details or the how and why, just list the emotions and identify on a scale of one to ten how easy it was for you to allow those emotions to flow through your heart. If you notice constriction around certain emotions, you can use the tools mentioned in the earlier chapters to make more space for your energy to flow. You don't have to "try" to love yourself. You will directly experience that you *are* love when the layers of protection begin to dissolve.

Your biotechnology is designed perfectly so that you must establish a truce with yourself before you can experience your potential. It is through the access point of self-love that you contact the higher aspects of yourself.

Be sure to journal your answers to the questions related to this energy center before continuing. It is essential to gradually build a solid foundation as you journey through your body.

In the next energy center, you will discover how your conditioning may be impacting your ability to bring your unique gifts into the world.

Chapter 6

"If you bring forth what is within you, what you bring forth will save you. If you do not bring forth what is within you, what you do not bring forth will destroy you." - Gospel of Thomas

Now that you have a better understanding of how your needs for physical security, relationships, individuality, and love can be met in a way that supports your healthy body and evolution, it is time to explore our need for freedom.

Hiding

Do you ever wish you were invisible?

My brother's closet was my favorite part of our 1100-square-foot, three-bedroom, one-bath ranch house. At first glance, it was just a simple closet, but if you looked back to the right, you could see that it extended behind the wall for another three feet. The section behind the wall always had a little empty floor space that was just perfect for hiding. I could squeeze in there with my knees against my chest and feel safe. I fantasized about hiding there when my father was raging. When anyone asked me what superpower I would like to have, it was "invisibility."

When my father was yelling, hitting us, and throwing things, hiding was not allowed. If he was angry, he was angry at everyone, and everyone had to be present and accounted for. The dinner table was probably the most dangerous place for things to go sideways. When he came home from work at 4:30 p.m., we all had to be at the dinner table. No excuses. A misinterpreted glance or wrong word could trigger an evening of terror. Just once, I wanted to get up from the table and hide in the back of that closet, but I never had that chance. Sitting at the table, I would keep my eyes down and my face blank. I was excellent at hiding my emotions, and I am grateful that my body had the innate wisdom to make me as invisible as possible. It was a good thing. There was just one problem—my conditioning to make myself invisible around angry people didn't stop when I moved out of my father's house.

I have carried that programming with me every moment of my life. As a nurse practitioner, when I could clearly see that survival adaptation patterns were causing people to be ill, I was too afraid to speak up. When I did challenge the narrative, it took very little pushback for me to retreat into silence and invisibility. While I was working in functional medicine, we learned how to do a "timeline." What I loved about the timeline was that it gathered not just a medical history, but life events, or triggers to illness. Finally, I had a medically approved tool to do the type of compassionate inquiry I knew was necessary.

I was working in a small private practice when I completed my functional medicine training and attempted to introduce the timeline to my colleagues and staff members. I was excited to give a presentation on the timeline. There were fifteen staff members sitting around the table on that August afternoon as I explained the benefits of taking this type of history that included clues about life events and conditioning. I carefully picked out my outfit for the presentation and put together my notes, handouts, and a slide deck.

About seven minutes into my presentation, my supervising physician interrupted me, "Lora, this timeline is no different than the medical history I have been doing my whole career. We will not be changing the way we are doing things around here." He was a smart man, my boss, and someone I respect. The survival conditioning immediately took me back to being eight years old at the dinner table with my angry father, and I felt my life force draining out of my body. I couldn't fight, and I couldn't run. I stopped speaking and maintained a calm expression. He was raising his voice, and his face was flushed. I scanned the faces of those around the table, and no one would make eye contact with me.

Later that evening, when I could calm down and think, I knew I needed to find a way to use my voice to speak the truth about what I could see was causing symptoms and illness. I had done enough work to know that I was not a victim; I was making a choice that was not in resonance with my health, and it was self-destructive. I began aligning with the truth that what I have to say does matter, and I have a purpose in life beyond taking orders from the scariest person in the room. I no longer have to be complicit in my own self-destruction in exchange for the illusion of safety and protection.

Transforming Survival Instincts

The conditioning of survival when someone cannot run, hide, or fight back is to "play dead," to make oneself as quiet and unanimated as possible in the effort not to trigger an attack. "Playing dead" was my automatic unconscious survival behavior, and it worked. That is the thing about our survival adaptations. For all our harsh judgments against them, we can't deny that they work or we wouldn't be here to complain about them.

What I knew was important patient information is popularly known to healthcare providers as a trauma history. This type of history taking would be the breadcrumbs leading to the excavation of the conditioning in the patient so that they could begin to access their power to heal. This paradigm shift is threatening to the healthcare system. If you have an entire culture of medicine built on keeping the patient endlessly fighting against themselves, and see a person's physical health as separate from their emotional health, then understanding their story and helping them access their power would be pointless. But in my personal experience and in the people I have worked with over my career, the whole story matters. What I see is that our conditioning always shows up in our lives, either in our bodies or our relationships, and usually both.

Unconscious persistent self-destruction for a long-past danger is an energy pattern I have seen repeatedly in myself and those I mentor. There have been several turning points in my life when I began to speak what felt true to me and beloved people in my life did not like it. They wanted me to go back to the way I used to be. Groups of people like the group members to follow the rules. It's kind of the whole point of being in a group. Nothing challenges the group like a member going through a transformation. There is physical safety in numbers, and sticking with a group is good for survival.

A few of the people who were at the meeting that day came to me in private later to offer their sympathy for what happened, but at the table, all were silent. This is how many groups work. If the group members feel threatened, afraid of losing a paycheck, relationship, title, approval, acceptance, or prestige, they will not speak. The programming works exactly as it is supposed to, and the group survives. Given that most of us want to be good people and we look to the group for cues on what is considered "good," the pain and potential power around this energy can be intense.

The Energy Center of Freedom

The fifth energy center develops between the ages of seven

and twelve. It relates to our ability to communicate and align with our unique gifts, and it challenges us to let go of the conditioning that keeps us craving security instead of expansion and transformation.

When your conditioning related to fear of speaking what you know to be true blocks energy from your body, this lack of energy gets passed down into your thyroid gland, and it operates at reduced effectiveness. One way it can respond is through decreasing the release of the triiodothyronine (T3) and thyroxine (T4) hormones. The purpose of these hormones is to tell the cells in your body how fast to work. If there is less T3 and T4 in your system, your whole metabolism slows down. Things like weight gain and fatigue usually follow a slowed metabolism.

This is your body gently pulling the reins on you because you are galloping in the wrong direction. Perhaps you do not feel aligned with your work anymore, are afraid to make a change, or feel you are not speaking your truth in your relationships. Your body will provide the information that you are out of alignment—first with emotions, then in physical imbalance, then in a dysfunction, and finally in a disease state. The guidance will first be a whisper and get louder depending on how receptive your mind is to the information.

Remember, the energy frequency must match the needs of the body in order for the organ to function correctly. In every moment, your cells are vibrating somewhere along the continuum of feeling completely liberated or feeling trapped by your circumstances. I have never met someone who has felt a complete sense of freedom in every moment. The body itself can feel like a prison if we are fighting against it. Your thyroid gland was not designed to operate at the energetic level of chronic survival conditioning.

When this center is malfunctioning, you can become overly talkative, self-righteous, and overbearing with a limited ability to be present and listen fully to another. A person can be resistant to change, unreliable in their words, or unable to communicate their ideas clearly. Somewhere between the heart and the mind, the signals are getting crossed, and words become weapons instead of tools. The first step in working with this energy center is becoming aware of the words that you are using.

In the healthcare system, they manage thyroid problems with pharmaceuticals. If you are lucky enough to see a more natural healthcare provider, they may advise you to take certain supplements or change your diet. While all these things may help with the symptoms, and eating a healthy diet is always a good idea, the inquiry needs to go deeper if you want to find the cause.

Your body *never* makes mistakes. Doing a self-inquiry with compassion and trust in yourself is a way to come into resonance. Your body will let you know when you come back into alignment. First your shoulders will soften, your teeth will unclench, your mind will clear, then your heart will softly open, and you will know that you have contacted the truth inside of you that wants to come through your voice. With each energy center, you can begin to employ this process of curiosity and awareness.

You may not necessarily feel happy, but you will feel expansion instead of constriction. Your energy and power will be flowing again.

The experience of feeling trapped and unable to speak creates the wound at this energy center. Like all of your energy centers, when the wound is created, a portal to finding the way back to your power is created at the same time. This is the doorway to accessing your freedom—when the light of consciousness is brought in. Most of us have understandably been afraid of our shadows and wounds, but this is the birthplace of our potential when we have the courage and support to lean into the discomfort.

For decades, I wanted to be "invisibly visible," like a shadow of a person, but not an actual person. I would find one successful person (usually a man), after another to hide behind, doing my work in the shadows with them getting the credit (and potential blame), thinking I was being good by staying small and quiet. Now I realize that all along I was the terrified child at my father's dinner table trying to be invisible, afraid of upsetting anyone, afraid that I couldn't handle the consequences.

The conditioning of not feeling safe to speak your ideas can stop you in your tracks. Those ideas may cause your family, friends, boss, religion, colleagues, or social group to reject you. In writing this book, every excuse came to my mind. "I don't know how to write a book. The world doesn't need another book. It is going to suck. People are going to know things about me that are embarrassing. People will have feelings, and I won't be there to manage them."

What kept me going was realizing that if I speak from a soft heart and a clear mind, I can trust that what I have to say matters. Even if it only matters to me and one other person on the planet, I matter and so do you.

There is a persistent fantasy that there is a way to be a human and have a pain-free life. The truth is that every human is terrified of their own power, and no one is getting a pain-free life. If we were not wired for survival and conditioned to fight the unfamiliar, then perhaps transformation would be easy. On this journey of remembering who you are, there is going to be pain, but there does not have to be suffering in the form of feeling sorry for ourselves or telling ourselves we are in pain because we are doing something wrong.

The paradox is that life becomes much easier when you are willing to take risks. We can compare it to going from rowing a boat against the tide and wind to harnessing the power of the wind with your sails. You are not trapped in needing constant reassurance that things are going to turn out a certain way because you know from experience that you can handle whatever happens. You have already survived a lifetime of unknown outcomes, and you are still here.

Because of the perfect design of the body and your energy centers, when the fifth energy center works well, it is in alignment with the truth of the first four centers. You realize you are abundantly supported, connected to all of life, cherished as an individual, and loved unconditionally. This is what your body has shown you to be true, and now you are free to share your unique gifts with the world.

Often those I work with are seeking to find their life purpose. The good news is, you don't have to "find your purpose." It's not lost and never has been. It is inside of you, like everything else you need. You arrived on planet earth fully equipped for your life mission. The task is to let go of what is *not* aligned with your body. You can do this by using all the tools we have discussed so far, along with other tools and resources you find from other mentors along the way. When you loosen the grip on your survival conditioning, your purpose will be right there, where it has always been. Once you see it, it will be so obvious that you will hardly believe that you couldn't see it earlier.

When your energy centers are flowing as intended, the fuel that your life purpose requires will be available. On some level, we all know that the purpose of life is a life of purpose. When we are not operating in the flow of our purpose, it bothers us because it is *supposed* to bother us. When you are no longer depleting your energy to "fight the enemy," your purpose will have the fuel that it needs.

As you go through the questions, stay in your body, and stay curious and friendly. Feel what makes your body relax, your mind clear, and your heart open. This is not an intellectual process; it is a practice of direct *knowing*.

When you *know* the truth, the truth will set you free.

Time to Get Curious

Here are some questions to "read" your body and beliefs related to your sense of freedom:

* What do you know about your life from the ages of seven to twelve?

- Are there people with whom you are afraid to verbally disagree?

- Do you seek to change others with your words, saying the same thing over and over?

- Can you express yourself honestly and openly?

- Are you feeling in alignment with your life's purpose?

- Are you able to sense when you are receiving guidance to act upon?

- What fears do you have about guidance from your higher self?

- Do you follow through on your creative ideas, or do you direct them into dead ends through distraction, numbing, drama, busyness, avoidance, or addiction?

- Do you have symptoms in any of these parts of your body: throat, thyroid gland, trachea, neck, mouth, teeth, gums, jaw, shoulder, neck, esophagus, or parathyroid gland? Do you have a slow metabolism or fatigue?

What to do:

As you are learning, when your body is stuck in "survival mode" because of prior life events,conditioned reactions for self protection will be automatic.This is why it is essential to work directly with the body and not just the mind in order to get your energy flowing. If you notice that your energy frequency needs an upgrade here, try this quick and easy exercise. Twice a day, ideally right before or after brushing your teeth. Gargle vigorously for 30-60 seconds. Gargling is so effective because it directly stimulates the vagus nerve which flips the safety switch in your nervous system. This is a simple, free and powerful tool to quickly change your frequency. If gargling seems too weird, humming and singing will also stimulate the vagus nerve, clear your fifth energy center and help your body feel safe.Try it and see how it works for you.

Be sure to journal your answers to the questions related to this energy center before continuing. In the next energy center, you will discover how your conditioning may be limiting your ability to have insight and respond creatively to the challenges in your life.

Chapter 7

"The fact is, people write their own self-destructive narratives, then try to pass the buck
to God or destiny." - Sadhguru

We are now at the head, having traveled and explored
throughout your magnificent biotechnology. I trust you
are feeling inspired and grateful for your equipment!

It is easy to get "heady" and disembodied as we enter the
energy centers of the mind, and if there is pain in our lives
and bodies, the seduction of escaping into fantasy is there.
Yet your power lies in being fully embodied, wanting to
inhabit exactly where you are, standing fully in the stable
pyramid of flowing energy that you have been cultivating
for yourself.

Medications Aren't Always the Answer

It took me quite some time to become more truly aligned with my body.

As a nurse practitioner indoctrinated in the promise of pharmaceuticals, my motto was "Better living through chemistry." The mid-'90s were the golden age of selective serotonin reuptake inhibitors, or SSRIs. Prozac was the holy grail solution for all those suffering from depression. Exhausted by my dark moods, social anxiety, and cyclical suicidal thoughts, and seduced by the promise of less emotional pain, I convinced my gynecologist to prescribe an SSRI for me. It helped some, but there were side effects. Luckily, the pharmaceutical companies kept creating new antidepressants for me to try. I just needed to keep experimenting until I found the right one. Finally I landed on one that had fewer side effects and minimized the dark times. Yes, I felt numb, and I had chronic stomach symptoms, but I was thinking about suicide less often, and life seemed to be a little easier. Busy with graduate school, being a wife, and mother to two daughters, I continued on it for a decade, but I never enjoyed depending on a pill every day.

Against the wishes of my husband, who had seen me at my worst, I weaned off. Life got harder when the numbness went away. Investing in alternative treatments like supplements, dietary changes, meditation, and exercise, I spent about eight years on no medication but regularly had nightmares, suicidal thoughts, meloncholy, anxiety, and difficulty maintaining healthy relationships.

In 2007, I began working in a psychiatrist's office prescribing mood-altering drugs by the dozens. I decided to actually see a psychiatrist for the first time in my life. He diagnosed me with "dysthymia," which is like a mild version of bipolar depression. It still surprises me that the psychiatrist did not ask enough questions to realize I was suffering from the impact of trauma. One of my best coping skills in life is to appear calm when I'm not, so I imagine that I was very difficult to assess. He prescribed a small dose of lamictal as a mood stabilizer. The side effects were minimal, and I noticed that my everyday life was not quite the struggle, but there was always something inside of me that wished I did not have to depend on a pill every day. I felt stuck. I had tried every diet, body work, hypnosis, therapy, sweat lodge, drumming, meditation, supplement, and prayer, and still I depended on a pill every day.

During a lunch break in early 2018, I was sitting in my car listening to talk radio when an interview with Michael Pollan discussing his new book *How to Change Your Mind* came on the station. It was the first time I had heard anything about the therapeutic use of psychedelics, and it fascinated me. I started reading everything that I could find on the topic. Given my strict religious upbringing and not having had the typical college experience, my most profound, mind-altering substance up to that point was a shot of tequila. I was quite surprised to discover twenty years of recent research and evidence that humans have been using mind-altering substances from the earth for thousands of years.

In 2019, I found my way to the Netherlands, where psilocybin-containing truffles are legal for a guided high-dose experience. There were twelve women and three guides in a group setting for a four-day retreat. What I experienced for the first time in my life was a nonprogrammed version of myself. The word "ineffable' is often used to describe a psychedelic experience, so I will not spend a lot of time trying to describe it, but in short, I had an embodied experience of safety that I had never experienced in my life. It was like my body was an instrument that had been playing out of tune since birth, and for a few hours, I got to experience it being played as it was intended and felt my own sweet resonance.

After that retreat, I had hope for the first time in my life that my childhood had not permanently damaged me. If an ugly little psilocybin-containing truffle could take me through a doorway inside myself, the doorway must have always been there, and I was going to access it. A few more high-dose psilocybin experiences combined with integration therapy, breathwork, and some regular psilocybin microdosing helped me, so within a year, I successfully was weaned from the mood stabilizer. For the first time in my life, I didn't have to take a pill every day, and I didn't have to live with persistent dark moods, nightmares, and suicidal thoughts.

You Are Not Broken

Most people probably won't have to go to the extremes of using a psychedelic substance, and I am not promoting the use of illegal substances. In full transparency, I wanted to share this part of my story with you. I would like to say that I could exercise, pray, diet, supplement, and meditate my way out of the impact of my life's events, but I needed the intelligence of the psilocybin to help me. It wasn't something that fixed me; it was something that allowed me to experience that I was not broken.

How do our (mostly unconscious) beliefs become our biology? What intelligence is in a psilocybin-containing truffle that communicated to my body so powerfully that it overrode decades of programming for a few hours? How is it that a handful of exposures to a naturally occurring substance could reset my nervous system in a way that taking a pharmaceutical every day for decades could not?

Throughout the book, we have been talking about beliefs and conditioning. Our beautiful brains make this conditioning possible. In today's society, we revere the brain. We spend thousands of dollars educating it, we reward it with grades, jobs, and material things. We rely on it to make decisions. Yet many wise ancestors have warned that the mind is a terrible master. Every spiritual discipline has as one of its primary goals a taming of the mind. What is it about our brain that seems to be our biggest evolutionary advantage, *and* the source of all of our suffering?

Remember, we all live in the world of our stories. Every story of my life that I have shared with you so far is simply that, a story. Yes, events occurred, but if you had lived these same events, the story you would tell would be different. If you were to ask my mother or brother about these events, their stories would be different. No matter what has happened to us, it is the story that we continue to tell ourselves about it in the present moment that will determine what that event means and what resonance our cells inhabit. It is with the brain that we realize we have the freedom to choose the story and, therefore, create the meaning of anything that happens to us.

The Energy Center of Creativity

The sixth energy center is between the eyebrows and connects to the pituitary gland within the brain. This center develops between thirteen to eighteen years of age. The pituitary gland is about the size of a pea. Although it is quite small, it either produces or stores many hormones: adrenocorticotropic hormones (ACTH), growth hormone (GH), luteinizing hormone (LH), follicle-stimulating hormone (FSH), prolactin (PRL), thyroid-stimulating hormone (TSH), antidiuretic hormone (ADH), oxytocin, and melanocyte-stimulating hormone (MSH).

The pituitary gland is often called "the master gland" because it regulates hormone activity in so many other endocrine glands and organs.

It stimulates:

The adrenal glands to produce the stress hormone cortisol.

Male and female gonads to release sex hormones, testosterone in men and estrogen and progesterone in women.

The production of male and female gametes (sperm and ova).

Growth of tissues and bone, as well as the breakdown of fat.

Breast development and milk production in women.

The thyroid to produce thyroid hormones.

Maintenance of water balance by decreasing water loss in urine.

Lactation, maternal behavior, social bonding, and sexual arousal.

Melanin production in skin cells called melanocytes, inducing skin darkening.

It is a great example of how all the systems in our body are perfectly connected. Many of the chemical messengers we have already discussed in the first five energy centers are under the influence of this gland.

In every moment, your cells are vibrating somewhere along the continuum of reacting in fear to external circumstances or creating from a place of internal security. It is the rare person who goes through every day from birth to death feeling completely secure in their ability to creatively respond to life's challenges. When the programming causes the energy frequency to consistently drop below what is necessary for the cells to function, then imbalance, symptoms, and eventually disease will occur in this area. It is a powerful shift to step out of reaction mode and take responsibility for what you are creating with your focused attention.

Your pituitary gland is designed to operate optimally at the energetic level of realizing your creative power and the impact of your thoughts on the material world. When you spend decades locked in unconscious beliefs of helplessness and reactivity, this master gland will have a negative impact on nearly all the other hormones in your body.

At the level of our brain, where our conditioning is governing our physiology, the influence of our beliefs is undeniable. One example would be symptoms of infertility in a woman. If a woman has been conditioned to believe that the world is dangerous with scarce resources, the pituitary gland in her brain is going to be sending a signal of danger and scarcity to the ovaries. Symptoms of infertility would be a natural response when viewed this way. It is a common phenomenon that a woman who gives up on conceiving adopts a child and then spontaneously gets pregnant. When she adopted the child, she had the experience of giving love unconditionally and her pituitary got the message the world is safe and abundant. I am intentionally oversimplifying here, but at the same time, when you understand how your body responds to your conditioning, you see that it is simple and precise.

Most of the time, we use the brain to imagine a future that is frightening. This is especially true if frightening events have occurred in your life, even if those events were long ago. This brain activity is typically not conscious, not realizing that the body only lives in the present moment. If you are thinking of something terrible, the body experiences it as a present-moment experience. Using real, present-moment resources to fight an imaginary enemy from the past is self-destructive and if this goes on for long periods of time, the body suffers. The body cannot override messages coming from the brain. It can only provide feedback. For example, the thyroid gland cannot tell the pituitary gland how to function. It can only provide information to the pituitary gland.

For all of its amazing abilities, the brain cannot directly perceive reality, which means it cannot directly perceive the present moment. The brain can only process the data gathered by the body and create a story. The body perceives present-moment reality, communicates this to the brain, and the brain creates a story. If the brain is missing data points, it will make things up just to have a complete story. This is an evolutionary advantage, *and* it is also a disadvantage because it can keep us stuck in outdated or false stories, like putting on a vinyl record from the '60s that is scratched, or playing an old eight-track tape instead of downloading a fresh, up-to-date version of a song. There is nothing wrong with listening to the "oldies," but too often we mistake the old tapes for present-moment reality. We get lost in old narratives, playing them over and over to the cells in our bodies. It requires discipline to update the programming. There are a variety of ways to decondition or discipline the mind. The most accessible is meditation, which is simply the decision to observe thoughts as they come and go in the mind. This is simple but not easy, especially in the beginning. When you become the observer of your thoughts, you will gradually realize that if you are able to observe your thoughts, then you are not your thoughts. You are the observer. This experience alone is transformative.

The brain is conditioned from birth to judge almost anything that is unfamiliar as a threat—to judge the unknown as bad. This is the root of nearly every dreadful thing one human has done to another—someone thinking they were being threatened by someone else. We can clearly see how essential it is to align our sixth energy center with the truth in our bodies. We cannot find our power or fuel our purpose when we insist on seeing everything uncomfortable or unfamiliar as the enemy that needs to be destroyed.

We live in a time where we have access to many weapons and escapes to deal with the uncomfortable. In actuality, most often things that are uncomfortable are an invitation to expand. We cannot transform or evolve without tolerating novelty, which, by its very nature, causes discomfort and an activation of the conditioning. The more "threatened" we think we are, the stronger the programmed response.

When people make up a story and raise their children to believe a version of reality, those children do not have a choice. They will align with their caregivers for survival. You can think of this as your "inheritance." The problem is not that we are conditioned. Being conditioned *is* the human condition. The problem occurs when we resist the truth coming through the body because it challenges the conditioning, and we cannot tolerate the discomfort of expanding into the unknown.

As it turns out, avoiding pain is good for pharmaceutical companies and those invested in keeping you trapped, disempowered, and dependent, but is a barrier to you experiencing your power and purpose. If you are willing to spend the pain that you have inherited on expanding your consciousness, then you access your birthright.

Fortunately, the truth cannot be programmed out of the body. It continues to exist in the present moment, perceiving reality. The mind can be put under a hypnotic spell of conditioning and amnesia, but the body cannot. This indeed, is our saving grace. For when the brain begins to trust the body more than the conditioning, we have an opportunity to be "saved," not from hell or damnation, but from our own self-destruction.

The brain is a storytelling device that has been conditioned to tell a survival story over and over. The survival story is an important and good story. We survived, but we didn't survive just to tell the survival story over and over. We survived as conscious beings so that we can have the opportunity to expand our consciousness.

Since our bodies are perceivers and holders of four billion years of intelligence, the opportunity is to train the brain to honor the body even when it conflicts with our programming. You have been learning how to honor your body with each of the exercises offered so far. Although this task can seem overwhelming, any effort or progress made will be well worth it.

With the body's ability to perceive the truth and the brain's freedom to create a story based on knowledge of support, connection, individuality, love, and freedom, you have the chance at creatively solving problems and expanding beyond reactivity.

Life is constantly transforming, and so are we, because we are part of life. Occupying the unique position of conscious citizens, we have the birthright to consciously take part in our own transformation when we are resonating with the intelligence available to us at every moment.

Time to Get Curious

Here are some questions to "read" your body and beliefs related to your intuition and insight:

- What do you know about your life from the ages of thirteen to eighteen?

- Do you easily feel victimized or have a sense of helplessness when faced with challenges?

- Do you have a vision of your life that is beyond survival or material gain?

- Are you able to see your patterns of reactivity in response to challenges?

- Have you developed an ability to access and trust your intuition?

- Do you have any of the following physical symptoms: depression, anxiety, frequent headaches, memory loss, hormone imbalance, neurological symptoms, loss of vision, or hearing?

What to do:

If you have identified that you are out of resonance in this area, I invite you to experiment with the following exercise. Think of an area in your life where you have been wanting something for a long time, but despite all of your best efforts, you have been unsuccessful. This can be with your health, finances, career, relationships, or any other area. Write out the sentence: "What I really hate about having (fill in the blank with what you want) is . . ." Keep answering this question until you identify your unconscious programming about having what you want. Once the programming is identified, creative solutions that have never occurred to you will effortlessly arise in your mind, and you will have the chance to respond to opportunities in a new way. Don't let the simplicity of this exercise fool you. It never fails to be powerful and revealing. Remember, just because you identify conditioning or programming, does not mean you are ready to let it go, but it does mean that your consciousness has expanded. The grip of hopelessness and helplessness will be loosened each time you challenge yourself to bring the narrative out of the unconscious mind.

Be sure to journal your answers to the questions related to this energy center before continuing to the final energy center in the body. If you have enjoyed excavating your unconscious programming in the energy centers so far, you are going to thoroughly enjoy the next one!

Chapter 8

"If we insist on keeping Hell, we shall not see Heaven: if we accept Heaven we shall not be able to retain even the smallest and most intimate souvenirs of Hell." - C.S. Lewis

Almost everyone wants to be a good person. I think this comes from the fact that we are by our nature "good." It also comes from believing that good people get what they want and bad people get punished. But who gets to decide what is good and what is bad? Most importantly, how can someone other than you decide what the intelligence who is creating you would identify as good or bad? So much of our conditioning comes down to not feeling good enough. Not good enough for God, parents, teachers, siblings, lovers, spouses, bosses, society, and so on. There seems to be a constant focus on some type of self-improvement which in its nature implies that we need to be improved upon.

In this final energy center, we step into the resonance of worthiness. Because we are conscious, we know that there is some type of creative intelligence that exists. Whether we identify this intelligence as God, the void, or simply the source of life, its existence is undeniable. In this energy center, we explore the impact of coming into conscious contact with that intelligence.

Heaven and Hell

In the Christian church in which I grew up, I heard the word heaven at least twenty times per week. They described heaven as a physical place far away that had pearly gates, mansions, and streets of gold. God would replace our sinful bodies with heavenly bodies, and we would float around with angels and never want for anything. On the other hand, there was hell. This was described as a fixed, eternal "lake of fire" where we would burn forever but never die. We focused nearly every aspect of our lives and our religious conditioning on how to get to heaven and avoid hell.

Another phenomenon that was frequently mentioned was the rapture. This was explained as an event where God would appear in the sky, blow a trumpet, and all the people who were "saved, or born again," alive or dead, would immediately be given a heavenly body that could fly to heaven in the sky. The people who were left on earth after the rapture would suffer. First the water would turn to blood, then they would have sores on their body, and eventually they would find themselves in hell, but not before they spent some serious time regretting that they had missed out forever on their chance to be saved.

One of our childhood weekend church activities was to drive into neighborhoods and walk door to door in pairs or small groups, handing out pamphlets warning people about hell and inviting them to come to church and be saved. These pamphlets had graphic pictures of people covered with boils while their bodies were burning. We were told that we should focus our every interaction with those who were not saved on trying to save them from hell. It was recommended that we carry our Bible with us to school because it was our responsibility to convert sinners and save them from this fiery fate.

As a child, I was terrified of hell. It was easy to assess the situation and see that I would never be good enough to go to heaven. I couldn't even be worthy of my dad's approval, so I was certainly not going to be good enough for God.

I lived in constant fear of the rapture. A few times a year when something troubling was happening in the world, the sermons became very heated, as the rapture was surely getting closer. God was coming any minute to rescue the good people from the bad ones. Sometimes someone in the church would stand up and give a chilling prophecy that it was indeed imminent. When I was at the grocery store with my mom and lost sight of her for a moment, fear gripped me. More than once, I went into the bathroom at the store to see if the water had turned to blood yet. We lived about seven miles away from the closest grocery store, and I worried about having to walk all the way home when my mother was taken in the rapture and they left me behind because I was not "saved." It was such a relief when I finally got my driver's license and didn't have to worry about walking home if the rapture happened while we were at the store buying milk and bread for the week.

Religious Beliefs

Some of this may sound silly to you, or maybe you grew up with a similar belief system. Sometimes it is easy to see where our conditioning may be self-destructive, yet other times it might be more difficult to see how so much of what we believe to be "true" or "accepted reality" as a society is our unconscious survival programming calling the shots. There are many examples of beliefs that our ancestors were willing to die for that would seem ludicrous to us now.

The idea of hell is an example of the type of narrative created by a threatened mind. It makes sense that a frightened, desperate person would create such a story so they could construct a way to feel in control by doing everything necessary to avoid hell. Yet what is the impact of believing that your creator could be so disappointed in you that they would dispose of you in a lake of eternal fire? This type of thinking combined is a setup for never feeling good enough and for staying stuck in a story of dependency.

What if there is a different story? What if the rapture or heaven is the natural outcome of a right relationship between the body and the mind when the mind trusts the body instead of ignoring it, controlling it, or judging it? What if the pearly gates to heaven are not far away or in a different body, but only accessible here and now in the body that you already possess?

The Center of Worthiness

In the body's seventh energy center, we find the pineal gland. This pine-cone-shaped structure the size of a grain of rice continues to develop throughout life. It primarily produces melatonin, which modulates sleep patterns and seasonal cycles. The pineal gland connects us intimately with the earth and plays an important role in regulating almost every function in your body: reproduction, executive function, growth, body temperature, blood pressure, sensory and motor activity, sleep, mood, and immune function.

Of all the endocrine organs, the function of the pineal gland was the last discovered, and to this day, there remains mystery around its true function. From the point of view of biological evolution, the pineal gland is a shrunken light receptor because it actually has rods and cones like the retina in your eyes. Philosophers throughout the ages believed the pineal gland to be the "spiritual eye." It has been theorized that this gland can produce N,N-Dimethyltryptamine (DMT), otherwise known as the "God molecule." This molecule is produced in certain circumstances such as birth, death, or near-death experiences, holotropic breathwork, altered states of consciousness, or when under the influence of psychedelic substances.

Unlike the vast majority of your brain, the blood-brain barrier does not isolate the pineal gland from the body.

It has a direct, abundant blood flow, second only to the kidneys, so it remains in direct contact with your body at all times.

Sadly, in modern times, the pineal gland is so commonly hard and calcified that it is used as a bony landmark on X-rays to determine if there is a space-occupying lesion in the brain.

The pineal gland allows us to access a bigger, broader, more advanced, intelligent view of the universe. This can be called "cosmic consciousness." Within your present-moment body, you have a receiver to contact the source of your life. This is your birthright as a human. You can call this source by any name that you choose, or no name at all, but you hold the technology for direct communication.

This goes beyond rational or intellectual thought, when the pineal gland becomes the receiver that it was designed to be. It allows for an awareness of who we are and of what we are capable.

At every moment, your cells are vibrating somewhere along the continuum of knowing you are worthy of being in conscious contact with your creator or feeling unworthy of such splendor. I have never met a person who has lived every day from birth feeling continuously worthy of being in communion with their creator. When your frequency consistently drops below what is necessary for the cells to function optimally in this center, imbalance, symptoms, and eventually disease will occur. Your pineal gland is open for conscious communion when it is bathed in the frequency of worthiness.

Activating the potential in this center changes everything. No longer do you see yourself as separate from life, but as a part of the fabric of the collective whole. You realize everything in your life is being created by you for the purpose of your continuous evolution. You begin accessing an understanding of the universe, how it works, and your place within it.

You *know* beyond an intellectual understanding that we are all one. That all of life is evolving together, and you have the opportunity to participate in your own unique way of being a part of conscious creation.

Moving through the six energy centers, you have exposed the programming created by experiences with family, religion, science, and culture—the programming that we are, to some degree, unsupported, alone, unwanted, unloved, trapped, helpless, and unworthy. Although you may have needed to adopt these beliefs at some moment in your life in order to survive, none of these things have ever been the whole truth about you.

When the energy comes up through all the energy centers and the light is turned on inside of your seventh energy center, you have walked through the pearly gates while still in your body. This is the journey that your body has been gently guiding you on since the moment of your first breath. When energy is flowing freely, at this energy center, your birthright of conscious contact with the intelligence that is creating you is realized.

Have you ever had the experience of owning an old smartphone, downloading an "upgrade" from the cloud and none of your old programs work any more? You can't find your contacts or even make a simple phone call. Something has gone awry between the cloud and your computer. They are not compatible and information is not accessible. You can use this understanding to explore the relationship between our bodies (the computer) and cosmic consciousness (the cloud).

It is a well-accepted fact that millions of inventions and discoveries have been made by two or more people in completely different parts of the world within weeks of one another. This is true for many things we use every day, like the microscope, photography, the thermometer, and air travel. When you apply the understanding of the cloud and the computer, you have a frame of reference for how multiple individuals can receive simultaneous downloads of the same information. If I do an internet search and find an answer to a question, I'm not inventing the answer. I'm downloading it through my computer. This is what is happening with us and cosmic consciousness. We are not "inventing" information, we are downloading it from the cosmic mind. The work of letting go of our survival programming and expanding our consciousness is how we prepare our computer to be compatible with the available data.

All the information needed for every invention is already in the cosmic mind. Think of inventors as those individuals who expanded their consciousness enough to allow for the download and also had the stamina to turn the idea into substance. That is what is available to you as your birthright. When you received a body, you received this potential; the potential to make contact with cosmic consciousness and be a channel for the cosmic to create something new through you. Stepping away from the analogy of the computer and the cloud, this cosmic mind is not something that is separate from you. It is the source that is creating you. The cosmic mind is seeking to become substance through your body. While we are fighting with our bodies, lost in our survival programming, cosmic consciousness is seeking to create through us.

While gaining access to cosmic consciousness may sound thrilling, by now you will understand how difficult it is to give up survival conditioning. The programmed mind thinks it needs to keep you protected by reminding you of how you have been hurt in the past and how you could be hurt in the future. In our personal and collective past, when we were dealing with actual external physical dangers, this type of conditioning was essential for survival. When facing the majority of our present-day problems, the survival conditioning of constantly perceiving threats instead of accepting the invitation to expand becomes a path of self-destruction.

We have become our own biggest threat because of our outdated programming.

Why is it so hard to let go of our beliefs? We are conditioned to judge anything that is painful as the enemy to be destroyed. Just as giving physical birth entails a lot of physical sensation, transforming or midwifing a new version of ourselves has a lot of sensation, and it is easy to feel threatened. Our conditioning is to label it, judge it, numb it, fight it, resist it, etc.

My invitation is to take your story, the story of how people didn't treat you right, how they cheated you, betrayed you, abandoned you, lied to you, hit you, took your stuff, or whatever the case may be, and realize they were operating out of their survival programming. A story of fear and lack conditioned them, and they were trying to survive. Let them off the hook, and let yourself off the hook at the same time.

Coming into the present, we realize life is constantly transforming, and so are we, because we are part of life. We have the unique birthright to consciously take part in creation when we are no longer fighting with ourselves and one another.

The "judgment day" was another threatening event that my childhood church preached about—when God would open a giant book where he had carefully documented all your mistakes, just waiting for the day to pull out the long list and judge you for all your sins. Now I have a different understanding of the "final judgment day." It is the day I choose to stop judging anything or anyone (including myself) as unworthy.

Does this seem impossible? To accept all of life, including yourself and all of those messed up humans around you, as worthy *right now*?

Why is it so difficult to stop judging the external as lacking when it is the perfect reflection of our collective consciousness? When you dig deeper on this one, you are bound to ask about all the horrible things that are occurring on planet earth at this very moment, believing only when these things have been repaired will it be okay to let go of judgment—only then can you stop fighting the enemy.

When you understand the law of cause and effect, you know that the physical or material world can only be the effect. The cause exists at the level of consciousness. It is only when our consciousness changes that the external world can change. It cannot be otherwise. Consider the analogy of the mirror. Think of the external world as the reflection, and consciousness is what is being reflected. As seductive as it may be to think that a change in the external (reflection) is the solution, this *never* works. This is true for each person individually, and for us as a species. When collectively our consciousness is in alignment with what our bodies remember to be true about us, the atrocities of the world will cease—not because we have finally defeated "evil," but because we realized we were only fighting against ourselves. When we can hold the consciousness of the truth that all of life is worthy, the terrible things we do to ourselves, each other, animals, and the planet will cease with no effort to change the external. The reflection will change because that which is being reflected has changed.

First, we will realize this in relationship with our bodies and stop seeing our "symptoms" as problems but as personal mirrors. Then we will see societal problems such as poverty, racism, disease, and violence as the reflection of our collective consciousness.

Where you are right now, experiencing whatever sensations you are experiencing, is a perfect reflection of your state of consciousness. Because of the design of the universe, it cannot be otherwise. When you observe the excuses arising to that statement, you will know where unworthiness is still present in you.

In case you are wondering. I personally have not achieved this as a constant state of being. I have disciplines that help me move into the present moment, into my body, and to be less resistant to changing the programming, but on any given day, I am riddled with judgment and resistance to what is happening. I, too, am constantly challenged by the habit of trying to change the reflection instead of what is being reflected.

My lack of perfection doesn't stop me from knowing who I am and what is possible. I know we are just beginning to embody our potential. As you are owning the power of your consciousness, I invite you to have daily disciplines that bring you back into resonance and that you allow yourself the support of others who are doing the same.

The End of This Physical Life

As sentient beings, knowing that we are going to die is something with which we have to cope. If during your life you have remembered who you are and have consciously taken part in your moment-by-moment expansion, it makes sense that you will be well equipped to trust the transformation that occurs at the moment of your last breath. Saying yes to the unknown will feel natural because you have been practicing. If you are still in the habit of resisting, fighting, distracting, and numbing yourself from the unknown, then you will most likely make the same choice at the moment of your transition from this body. This is the potential human path of experiencing eternal life through staying conscious at the time of death so that you will be conscious when you step into whatever comes after this incarnation.

To end this physical life knowing that you have shared your unique gifts, the gifts that no one before you or after you will ever be able to share, is your portion of heaven that you will leave on earth.

Time to Get Curious

Here are some questions to "read" your body and beliefs about worthiness.

- What events have occurred in your adult life that have challenged your belief in a benevolent creator?

- How would you describe your relationship with cosmic consciousness (God, nature, the universe, etc.)?

- Do you have grand inspirations or ideas but lack the energy to materialize them?

- What are your beliefs about life after death?

- Do you believe that there is a higher consciousness that disapproves of you, or seeks to punish or destroy you?

- Are you waiting for something or someone outside of you to "save" you?

- Do you believe you are worthy of heaven at this very moment?

Have you experienced direct contact with cosmic consciousness?

What to do:

If you have identified that this is an area in need of expansion for you, I invite you to create your own image of the intelligence that is creating you. Many people spend their lives unconsciously feeling unworthy of direct communion with their source, but that comes from believing that they are falling short in some way. No one enjoys being judged and punished. Invest a few minutes each day to imagine being held in the gaze of a power that is creating you as you are for the purpose of communion with you. Allow yourself to experience that you have always been and always will be perfect in the eyes of your creator. Most people do not have a religious figure that they feel approves of them completely as they are, but if you do, use the image that you feel comfortable with.

You may go back through the energy centers as many times as you wish. Each time, there will be new revelations and your consciousness will continue to expand. Your body will be your trustworthy companion every step of the way.

Final thoughts for the reader

"All sickness is homesickness." - Dianne M. Connelly

Congratulations! You took the spectacular journey through your body and learned how magnificent your biotechnology is. Having the gift of a body which allows you to expand your consciousness is a priceless treasure. This way of thinking about yourself may be new, so be patient with yourself.

Saying yes to the disowned parts of yourself that you may have spent your lifetime unconsciously avoiding is not for the faint of heart. As you discovered in your process, moments of pain are unavoidable. Expansion of consciousness is a return to wholeness. This wholeness may look like a peaceful, conscious death, resolving an illness, or something else entirely. Whatever your path, your body is the perfect technology for the expansion that is available throughout your life.

Through your wounds, you can access your power and your purpose. But you are the only one who can choose to approach the door and walk through. Trusting the changes when all of our conditioning has been geared to avoiding or resisting the unknown is the ongoing invitation for all of us. This is the human condition—terrified of change and designed specifically for conscious evolution.

We can't have it both ways—complaining in the back seat about where we are going while we refuse to get into the driver's seat. As children, we can't drive. We can't reach the pedals. We don't know the rules of the road, and we don't have a license. At some point, we are big enough to sit in the driver's seat and take responsibility for our destination. Your body is the vehicle for where you are going. It is the only vehicle that you are going to have in this lifetime, so understanding what it is communicating to you is a must.

The biggest human tragedy is to live one's whole life unaware of your birthright. Our fear of pain and discomfort can keep us from living connected to our bodies, hearts, and potential. We can blame our conditioning, parents, or society, but at any moment we also have the option of taking responsibility for ourselves. We have the capacity to transcend out of survival conditioning while being in our bodies—to become reconditioned, and for our cells to vibrate at a frequency that is compatible with life no matter what has happened up until now.

People have, throughout time, fallen for the false promise that liberation comes from escaping your body, but when you understand your technology, you understand that liberation is an embodied experience. It is no accident that the portal to liberation is only accessible through coming into alignment within the body.

Future

Artificial technology is here to stay, and in many ways it is superior to human biotechnology. Artificial intelligence doesn't get tired, make math errors, need food and shelter, struggle with addictions, worry, binge on Netflix, or waste energy on dead-end relationships. But human biotechnology has something that artificial intelligence will *never* have. We are plugged into the fabric of life and can consciously dance with life itself. The intelligence humming in our cells is constantly being updated. In order to excel and coexist with artificial intelligence, we are being invited to step into the potential within our biotechnology. Artificial intelligence will play its role, and we can partner with it to accomplish more, but it can never replace our biotechnology. It is up to us to use our instrument as it is meant to be used so we can have a balanced partnership with artificial intelligence.

Although I have heard of people who wake up from their conditioning 100 percent and stay awake, that has not been my experience. For me, it has been small awakenings followed by setbacks, like a three-steps-forward, two-steps-back process. It is a lot like peeling an onion (including the crying part). One day, I can experience a big-picture view and be celebrating my progress, and the next day, I can be feeling the pain and be tempted to fight it or reach outside of myself for relief. That being said, I have walked through enough pain with others that pain itself holds a place of deep reverence for me now. There is a part of me that can stay hopeful during the labor because I know the terrain. Something new is being born. The pain is temporary and minimal in comparison to the ecstasy of creation.

My journey has been made possible by many soul companions, my journal, beloved books, nature, my dogs, numerous therapists and healers, and long walks outside. I have come to understand that surrounding myself with people who are also committed to their own conscious evolution is essential. If I spend time with those who reinforce their victim story, I can get seduced back into feelings of helplessness, hopelessness, and resistance. I can easily begin using my energy to fight the enemy and forget that I am only fighting with myself.

It has been well over a decade since the death of my sister. I often think about the person she could have been, and am grateful for all she inspired in me. She is gone, dear reader, but you are still here. I invite you to make peace with your body and realize the magnificence of who you are. You are not broken, helpless, or hopeless. Whatever your story has been up to this moment, your birthright is to write the rest of your life's story and to live with a full awareness of who you are. There is limitless power and a unique purpose inside of you.

I trust that you have enjoyed this journey and have invested in yourself by pondering the questions at the end of each chapter. Maybe you have tried some of the tools that have been so beneficial to me and those with whom I have worked. Simply becoming aware of how your stories and beliefs impact your body is a huge step in the right direction. I invite you to keep using these tools as you embody more of your power and purpose.

Most importantly, I want you to know that *you*, as you are right here, right now, are exactly as you are supposed to be. You are supported, connected, wanted, loved, and liberated. You have always been, and always will be, worthy.

For more resources, I invite you to join my online community and check out my course of self-study. I also work with clients privately and collaborate with teachers and guides around the world.

For more information, visit my website:
www.lorasolomon.com.

Would you help?

Love this book? Don't forget to leave a review!
Every review matters, and it matters a *lot!*
Head over to Amazon or wherever you purchased this
book to leave an honest review for me. Your review will
help others in their journey.

Thank you so much.

Made in the USA
Columbia, SC
14 May 2022